Perfect Connections

MEMOIRS OF AN
AME
MINISTER'S WIFE

Marguerite Tiggs Birt

702 Birchwood Rd
Savannah, GA 31419

Copyright © 2003 by Marguerite Tiggs Birt

Printed by Lewiscolor Printing, Statesboro, Georgia.

ISBN: 0-9727613-0-6
Library of Congress Control Number: 2002096300

Dedication

To Amanda Lucille Birt

7/23/03

Dear Sister Callie,

Thank you for your leadership in missionary service. I hope you will enjoy reading and reflecting.

With appreciation,
Marguerite J. Birt

I

Contents

Forward

This ten-chapter volume, *Perfect Connections: The Memoirs of an A.M.E. Ministers' Wife* is a testament to the value of a strong Christian family life. Reading about the romance, relationship, ministry, trials, and successes of the Birt family will be an example to other husbands and wives. A love such as the one they shared is rare and beautiful. The Cummings' team strongly recommends *Perfect Connections: The Memoirs of an A.M.E. Ministers' Wife* as a must read for couples wanting to make a lasting difference in the challenging task of kingdom building.

Unparalleled in her dedication to education, Marguerite teaches and guides young wives by candidly sharing her life experiences. Her lessons learned and shared for the benefit of others show her sweet love of God, her adoration and respect for her husband, and her compassionate concern for others through her undeniable loyal service to the A.M.E. Connectional Church. What an incredible couple with an incredible story to share with God's people who are ready and willing to follow the holy spirit to **"Do God's Work, God's Way!"**

Frank C. and Martha C. Cummings
Bishop - Sixth Episcopal District
African Methodist Episcopal Church
September 2002

Acknowledgements

This book was edited by Charles J. Elmore, Ph.D., professor of humanities at Savannah State University. A Georgia and Savannah archivist, this historian and meticulous researcher is a prolific writer with several books to his credit. I am grateful to this southern gentleman for his assistance which surpassed my expectations.

Verdelle Lambert reviewed my manuscript with a journalists' eye. Reverends Winton Hill III, and Albert D. Tyson, Jr. reviewed this work as well. I am indebted to each of them for their comments and encouragement.

Appreciation is expressed to Reverend O'Neil Mackey, Sr. for writing the heartfelt Epilogue.

I sincerely thank Bishop and Mrs. Frank Curtis Cummings for contributing the Forward to my book. I am happy to live in Savannah now and to serve under their Episcopal leadership once again.

Finally, I thank God for everything.

Reverend and Mrs. Millard D. Birt

PREFACE

Perfect Connections: Memoirs of an A.M.E. Minister's Wife was in the making long before I picked up a pen to write the words. As I was being shaped by life, so was this book. Please do not misunderstand me. I am not saying that I am writing now because my formation is complete. This book will end, but my journey to personal growth will continue until I die. I asked myself, why was I writing, and could not answer myself. Only now, are the answers clearer.

First, I needed to write this book for me. The words that I searched for became the symbols that best expressed my thoughts. I struggled to match the words to my thoughts, and in the process became more aware of my identity. I struggled to put the words into sentences, the sentences into paragraphs, and paragraphs into chapters. In time, I recognized an order to my life...not orderliness, but sequential stages in which there were profoundly related patterns.

Second, I wrote this book for others. It is not intended to tell others what they must think or how one must behave to get results in one's life. This is not a blueprint for anyone. I would be satisfied if one could recognize in me some of the strengths, and limitations that one sees in themselves. Maybe, readers of this book will recognize the ingrained determination, episodes of adaptability, and the desire to have it all, which include a career, being a preacher's wife, a mother, a stepmother, and a child of the King. I ask the reader, can you see any of you, in me? Without me really knowing those who read this book, on a personal level, there is a deeper knowing that connects us because of the similarities and differences between our separate journeys. Lastly, I was compelled to tell my testimony about God's goodness. I have a new story to tell, and it is mine... all mine.

In chapter One, when *Perfect Connections* begins, it is at the end of my first marriage. That ending opened a new door... another beginning in my life. I did not get married that summer, in 1963, to divorce ten years later. There I was, single, and determined to start over by taking one day at a time.

In retrospect, the real beginning was being the last born of James and Lucille Tiggs, in 1939, in Savannah, Georgia. Daddy joined the army in 1942 when I was three. He went overseas, fought in World War

II, returned home, and admitted himself into a veteran's hospital in Maryland, remaining a patient there for seventeen years. Mom became the head of our household nurturing three daughters and a son; Sarah, Emma, James, and me. Everything she said to us, everything she did with us, to us, and for us, were our earliest and deepest roots.

Our relatives and neighbors, people in our church, our teachers, the friends we had, their parents, the things we did, the places we went, became as links in a chain. Where the links connected is where the strength of people's resources were invested to help us better ourselves.

Our cousin, Tadpole, teaching our brother to play golf is a link. Fannie Jenkins, exposing me to Claflin College, is another link as well as Mom and Daddy's enduring marriage. By the grace of God these links were strong, secure, and extended.

Reverend Millard Delano Birt and I met in 1974 and courted for two years. We accepted the twenty-one year age difference between us. The more we talked, the more we discovered that our paths connected in spite of our ages and life experiences. A friend once asked me, "Are you marrying an older man, because you're looking for a father figure?" I laughed. If I could have a husband, like my father, it would be all right with me. We married in 1976 with great expectations of learning from each other. He taught me about the power of faith in God. I taught him that my independence released him to make better use of his energies. It freed him as a man more than it liberated me as a woman. We were one, yet separate and unique. Our goals were similar. When there was nothing to do, we enjoyed doing nothing together. We brought tears of laughter to each other's eyes, and tears of happiness from the gentle way we loved each other. We loved God, and believed our paths crossed for a reason.

Millard's calling to the ministry was built upon his faith in God, his desire to serve God completely, and his commitment to lead others to Christ. He was my minister. I observed his steadfast faith, his service to others, and his reverence for God's power. Sometimes, I reminded myself, "My minister, is my husband." His life as my minister, and my husband, compelled me to draw closer to God.

My calling as an educator became richer because of my yearning to go see things for myself. Traveling, to study and interact with people from cultures in different parts of the world helped me to value peace. As an early childhood teacher, I became more responsible for passing on to children a love for peace. When the learners were adult college students, I passed to them the understanding that the way we rear children can determine whether we have war or peace within ourselves, in our homes, and in the world.

2

Our mother was a peacemaker. Mom had a way of saying "Come on!!" when we told her we were coming to Savannah, she and Millard became more than in-laws. When we visited, she made certain that we experienced the political, social, and economic progress of Blacks in Savannah. Mom and Millard had a zest for life, like two innocent children. She delighted in showing him a "new Savannah" that was quite different from the Savannah he knew decades ago as a boxer, and the one she knew as a school girl and young Army wife.

As an AME minister's wife, I knew I would always go where my husband was sent to pastor. I wanted to see his face in the morning, and see his face before I closed my eyes at night. I would be the trailing spouse, and learn more about the dynamics of moving and the effects upon the entire family. The subject had held my interest for years; so much so, my doctoral dissertation was about transience and its connection to the academic and social development of school children.

The years of observation and research on the subject of mobility, sustained me and provided insight as the Birt's became a more mobile family moving to New York, then to Connecticut. As time passed, we did not stop to think how much we were changing. The things that each of us experienced helped us to grow. The growth was occurring in different ways, and at different intervals in our lives. Our marriage unit was changing, and our family unit was changing. The most consistent thing was that things were changing.

The AME church was always at the center of our growth. All of the women's sessions at Dover, Delaware, the Learning Experience in Wilmington, the Minister's Wives and Widows Alliance meetings, the retreats, annual conferences - these settings educated me, committed me, and strengthened me.

The Young People's Department (YPD) is powerful in its training. We encouraged our daughter Amanda's participation with this organized body. She grew up in the church and the Educational Congress in Dover, and was in the audience the day, Reverend Delores Jacobs preached, "Knowing When to Leave the Party." She and her young friends did not know what we were all shouting about that day. However, she was growing in her understanding of praising God.

As Millard began to experience complications from the diabetes, it disturbed him when he could not be in the pulpit. He knew his illness altered his ability to pastor with the same success he once had. He must have been torn between holding on to his faith that his health would get better, and holding on to his integrity by stepping down so "the work of the church could go on…" He had to decide between staying, or stepping down.

I will never forget the day we were sitting on the front porch of the parsonage in Greenwich. Amanda was expressing her concerns about moving. He said, "You can … move anywhere in the world, make new friends, accomplish new things, but you must not ever move away from God. STAY CONNECTED TO GOD, THAT IS WHAT REALLY MAT-TERS."

When he asked Bishop Cousin on the floor of the 1995 session of the New York Annual Conference "… to send a pastor to Emanuel who is well …," he had made the decision to leave the (New York) party. He might have been afraid that day, but he did a brave thing. I was thankful to God for empowering him.

In the last chapter, we move to Greenwich, Connecticut, where Millard was assigned to pastor Bethel. From the outset, we experienced a peace there that passed our understanding. Millard gave his best to the church, and the church gave its best to us. After pastoring for over fifty-five years in the AME church, he said over and over "… Bethel is the sweetest part of my ministry…"

On Valentine's Day, in 1997, nearly twenty months after serving at Bethel, Reverend Millard D. Birt, my beloved husband, died, and went gently into that good night.

CHAPTER 1

The best place for me to begin is after my first marriage ended...

ONE DOOR CLOSES

On a snowy January day, in 1972, my first husband flew from Newark, New Jersey, to the Super Bowl. That same day movers came to our duplex home on a quiet tree-lined street, and loaded their van with boxes I packed weeks earlier.

"Lady," one of them said, "We move'em in, we move'em out, and we move'em back in again. We know by the way you packed, you not comin' back... so just take one day at a time."

I moved into an apartment at 1053 Madison Avenue in Elizabeth near the Newark city line. This way I was closer to attending Hopewell Baptist Church in Newark, where my husband and I worshiped for over ten years. He was a trustee, and I was a missionary.

After a year, I received a New Jersey no fault divorce and left for a trip to Jamaica on Flight 7022.

Soaring out of the turbulence, above clusters of gray clouds, I whispered, free.

"Excuse me," the lady beside me asked.

"FREE," I repeated

"AT LAST," she smiled.

I rested my head against the seat, remembered Montego Bay, and my first trip there as a newlywed. This time will be different I thought to myself, now I am single and alone.

The flight was filled with a group of New Jersey bowlers joking loudly with each other. They had seen me standing on the tarmac watching the baggage crew place my ten-speed bike on the plane.

"Miss, can you ride that thing?" one of them asked.

"I sure can."

After we landed, I boarded a jitney with my bike and suitcase. During the ride to the hotel I began to notice the countenance of people standing along the road. Their faces looked drawn. I knew that Michael Manley of the Peoples' Nationalist Party was prime minister of the newly independent Jamaica. He was establishing socialist policies and favored non-alignment with the U.S.

"Miss, I see you bought a plumb chicken, how much did it cost?," I asked a lady standing beside me on the crowded bus.

"I paid $6."

Jamaicans were struggling.

Upon arriving at the two-story yellow stucco hotel, I locked my bike to a safety stand. The grounds were wet from a light rain and smelled of jasmine.

"Nice," I sighed.

A catnap was all I needed before leaving the hotel and peddling away. As I rode further ahead, I saw a booth with woodcarvings.

"Anybody here?" I yelled.

"Yuh, mahn," the artist answered from the back where he was cooking in the bush. He offered me lunch and I accepted a piece of blackened fish. Without bartering, I paid Jared what he asked and deserved for two of his finely made carvings.

That first night in the hotel dining room, the maitre'd seated me beside an open veranda. As I looked out, I saw a white lattice gazebo with a group of steel band musicians dressed in fuchsia shirts playing my favorite song - "The First Time Ever I Saw Your Face."

Tears ran down my face as I wondered, what am I doing in a resort alone?

"Lovely evening, Madame, I'm Nigel."

The waiter popped open my napkin and covered my lap with it.

As I finished eating, the Jersey bowlers waved, and I left.

The next morning, as planned, Jared arrived on a black Yamaha motorbike. I paid for gas, and we sped off. After a while on the road, I relaxed my hold around Jared's narrow waist.

"I'll give you a sweet ride," he promised.

Descending southeast from Montego Bay, we passed the town of Reading, then Montiplier, and arrived at Cambridge in cockpit country. There are massive limestone formations there, which are deep depressions in the earth. At times, the elevations were so high, I was afraid to look down.

The road was narrow. There was hardly space for one vehicle on it, and when ascending traffic approached us on the right, horns tooted wildly. Each time Jared steered to the rim of the road I closed my eyes. I was scared and getting angry with this stranger for driving too fast. Finally, I spoke up for myself.

"I don't like riding fast, so please STOP!"

On the return, the ride was sweeter. He took me to visit his sister, who lived far in the hills away from the road. He chopped down a coconut from the tree beside her house and split it open with a machete. The coconut milk was cloudy and surprisingly cool. The visit was nice, especially when I met Jared's thirteen-year-old niece. She said she wanted to become a nurse, and asked me to send her a pair of sneakers. Soon after returning to Elizabeth, I kept my promise and mailed the sneakers to her without a return address. It felt good to be home.

Months later, in pouring rain, I drove from my apartment up Madison Avenue looking for a church. I saw Union Baptist Church on my left, where Reverend Jesse W. Mapson, Jr. pastored, and I decided to go there, but the parking lot was full. Ahead, on the right, was another church set back from the sidewalk with a platform in front of it and an empty parking space in plain view.

Inside, the sanctuary had stark white walls and red-carpeted floors. The exposed ceiling beams were of rich mahogany. The minister's head shined like a bronze dome above the podium, where a huge Bible was opened. Two women dressed in black robes were seated on either side of him. Then he stood up. He looked so huge. He was dressed in a black robe trimmed in red piping with a white clergy collar. He held a miniature gold cross in his massive hand, and it swayed on a slender gold chain. His tenor voice resonated as he and the congregation sang, "How Great the Wisdom." I had never heard this beautiful hymn before.

The women and tenors sang, "…The work is all divine…" Then, the men and altos repeated the refrain. I watched the minister's clenched fist rise in the air. At that, the whole church shouted in harmony, " THE WORK IS ALL DIVINE!!!" It was July 1974, and I was in Greater Mt. Teman AME Church, 160 Madison Avenue at its 11:00 morning service, where Reverend Millard Delano Birt pastored. His sermon was "Living One Day at a Time," the same advice the movers had given me.

As he preached, he threw his head backwards and gave little yells. He stretched out his arms, then covered his chest with them, and rocked himself in his own arms. He wiped dripping sweat from his head and face with a small white handkerchief. He pounded the Bible, arched his back far backward, and sang, "…My hope is built on nothing else than Jesus blood and righteousness…" Everyone was standing, praising God and singing, "…On Christ the solid rock I'll stand, and all other ground is sinking sand. All other ground is sinking sand…"

I walked to the offering table and there on the front pews were the bowlers on flight 7022: Morris and Ada Sykes, Henry and Rose Tucker, William and Jean Smith, Julius and Shirley Hunter, Harry and Marie Allen. I looked and saw the faces of others who had been on the plane,

Mt. Teman was their church. Before closing, Reverend Birt said, "You know we're opening a day care center in the church. We need someone with a degree in early childhood to be a consultant." After the service, I went to his office and offered my help. Two weeks later, I joined Mt. Teman. I was placed on Ruthie McNeil's class.

From L-R: Reverends Reginald McRae, Mary N. Garner, Edna Vaughn, Millard D. Birt

I continued tithing ten percent of my salary and was blessed to buy a two-family duplex in Savannah, Georgia, which I rented out. The house became a good investment for me, and I decided to return to graduate school for my doctorate. It was time to move ahead.

One Wednesday night, after Bible study, we were standing on the church porch - Reverend Edna Vaughn, Reverend Nina Garner, Reverend Birt, Luther Miller, the pastors' steward, Reggie McRae, and myself.

Reverend Birt said, "I'm going to Philadelphia, and if anyone wants to come for the ride, that would be nice."

"I'll ride with you Reb,' said Mr. Miller.

There was silence.

When I reached my apartment, Reverend Birt called and repeated himself.

Annoyed, I said, "Are you asking me to go to Philadelphia with you?"

"If you want to," he answered.

Two days later it was just the two of us riding on cruise control to Philadelphia on the New Jersey Turnpike in his 1974 blue Lincoln. There was a button in that car for everything. I used one to open my window to let out the smoke from his imported Murchion pipe. This was our first of many dates. Reverend Birt told long and colorful stories. I paid close attention, because, unlike him, when I told stories, I forgot the punch lines. One of his jokes was about "urine." I often asked him to repeat it just to hear him say, with indignation, "...BUT WHOSE?" Sometimes we would laugh until we cried. He was fun to be with, and was twenty-one years older than me. We had much to learn from each other, and we started out by laughing.

Philadelphia, Pennsylvania is the official residence during the eight-year tenure of the bishop of the First Episcopal District of the AME Church. The district includes churches in New England (Connecticut, Rhode Island, New Hampshire, Massachusetts, Maine), New Jersey, New York, Eastern Pennsylvania, Delaware, and Bermuda. Bethel African Methodist Episcopal Church is called the Mother Church. It is located at 419 Richard Allen Avenue on the original plot where Reverend Richard Allen and the band of freed and enslaved Africans met to worship after they walked out of St. George Methodist Church when their white church brothers rushed them from praying at the altar. Mother Bethel is reported to be "... the oldest parcel of real estate continuously owned by black people in America." The group left and founded The African Methodist Episcopal Church in 1816.

On one of our trips there, Althea, Cecelia, and Luther – three of Millard's four children, came with us for dinner at Bookbinders. I already met Lewis, the youngest, who lived with his father, and was a senior at Elizabeth High School. My kids, as Reverend Birt called them, were his and Lois' pride and joy. He and Lois were divorced in May 1974. After dinner we returned to their Cedar Street house where Reverend Birt had lived with his family before moving to New Jersey.

"My kids will always have a place to stay," he said to me. He bit on the stem of his pipe and his jaw muscles tightened. I could see his sadness as they walked away and closed the door of their house.

Mt. Teman's annual Women's Day is a high morning service with the crowning of Ms. Mt. Teman at the afternoon state rally program. Ruthie McNeil was Georgia's captain and the reigning queen for the past two years, having raised more money than South Carolina's captain, Dollie Harris. The competition is year round with novel fundraisers and warm fellowship.

"Ms. Grant, will you pour tea at our Georgia Tea?" Mrs. McNeil asked.
"What else do I have to do?" I asked.

"Not a thing, but pour tea."

The tea followed service, and was at Olivia Douglas' spacious home. I was seated at the head of the white lace covered table set with bone china and assorted finger sandwiches on silver platters. To my surprise, they seated Reverend Birt at the opposite end. He poured coffee from a matching silver server, holding it daintily in his hand, with his big pinkie sticking out. We were being shown off at the tea party to nearly fifty people, and Mrs. McNeil was the matchmaker. The kids were not in town this Sunday, and I was glad. This might have been a bit much for them.

Months later, after just returning from a conference in Los Angeles, Ruthie called.

"You know Revren' is having eye surgery tomorrow."

I hurried to the parsonage, next door to the church, and there in the living room, Reverend Albert D. Tyson, Jr., (Mt. Pisgah AME Church, Jersey City) was praying with Reverend Birt. I stood still in the foyer in reverence watching the two of them in prayer.

The surgery was for pterygium, a type of cataract. Afterwards his eyes were covered, then a week later only one. Naturally, he had a story to tell:

"I could see out of the good eye," he began. "My body was on a table and a smaller table was beside my head. They took my eyeball out of the socket and scraped my eye, then they put it back in."

"Did you feel anything?" I cringed.

"Are you kidding? My whole face was dead, just like it was the last time I boxed in the ring. Come to think of it, it was in Savannah. This guy knocked me in so many places in my face I had lumps everywhere. The next morning, when I looked in the mirror, I knew I would never box for money again. Three days later, I stood on the Savannah side of the Talmadge Bridge and hitched a ride with a man from Sanford, Florida. I ended up riding with him to a migrant camp in King Ferry, New York, and stayed there the whole summer picking beans."

" You won't believe this, in 1959, when I was at Savannah State College, my friend Drucilla and I worked for the summer in the New York Migrant Child Care Program in King Ferry too," I said to Reverend Birt.

I continued, "Can you understand why those people travel all the way up north to work in a migrant camp? Their children miss so much school. Once, the nurse came to give health exams in the nursery and she pulled a tapeworm from a baby's nose…it could have choked the baby to death. We have seen toddlers pass worms in their stool. I don't understand."

"There's more to it than what you see, Marguerite. You don't know where they come from… some of them think they're better off in a migrant camp. At least they get help they can't afford back where they live. You'd be SHOCKED at what people do to better themselves.

CHAPTER 2

There is an earlier beginning for me than what I have written at this point. While we were growing up, we were taught the difference between trying to be better than other people and trying to better ourselves. I need to begin there.

BETTERING MYSELF

Our father, James Hill Tiggs, was born in Augusta, Georgia, in 1914, and our mother, Lucille Butler, was born, in 1916, in Savannah. They met while they were in high school when Daddy moved from Augusta to live in Savannah with his Aunt Tata. They married, in 1931, afterwards Sarah, Emma and our brother James were each born two years apart, and I was the last to be born in1939.

When Daddy joined the Army in 1942, I was three years old. I remember us crying and hugging him under the big oak tree in our backyard. Our dog, Brownie, kept circling Daddy's legs until he finally patted his wagging tail. Later, Daddy was sent overseas to fight in World War II, then it was just Mama and us. She taught us how to iron, wash clothes, clean the house, and cook. Mom had a slender shape and wore her long hair in an upsweep pompadour. When we shopped downtown on Broughton Street, a white photographer always wanted to take our picture. Mom received a monthly military check for herself and one for us. To make ends meet, she did day's work and sold women's clothes door-to-door for a New York catalog company. We lived on Fifth Street, on the east side of Savannah.

Mr. & Mrs. Frank Callen (he started the Boys Club in Savannah, in 1917), lived at the corner of Wheaton and Fifth Streets. Mr. & Mrs. Smith lived to the left of the Callens. Mr. Smith was a teacher in Savannah, and Mrs. Smith, his wife, for whom Pearl Lee Smith School was named, was the first licensed female African American pharmacist in Georgia. Mrs. Smith worked at the Fonvielle's Savannah Pharmacy on West Broad Street, the only Black-owned pharmacy in Savannah.

A dirt lane separated their large corner houses from the row of

James Hill Tiggs

Lucille Butler Tiggs and
Marguerite on Broughton St.
Age 4
1943

wood framed houses where we lived. The Frank Loadholts and their children Francis, and Frank (Sonny) lived across the lane from the Callens. My sister Emma and Sonny were sweethearts and liked to climb china-berry trees together. Sarah teased her, "You're just a tomboy." The Robert Patrick's lived across the lane from the Smiths. They had four children our ages, and we played together. We did not know that Tommy Smalls was an important man when he came to visit the Patrick's pretty, light-skinned niece, "Gladys," whom Mr. Smalls later married. They opened the famous Small's Paradise in Harlem on 135th Street and 7th Avenue, in New York.

At the end of the street, Mr. & Mrs. Lawrence Warren lived in a house with steep concrete steps. From their elevated porch, we could really see "the bottoms" where several shanties made of wood, rags, and rusty pieces of tin were pushed out of sight under overlapping bushes. Bearded black men with long matted hair lived there. We called it tin city and dreaded seeing them. Mom said, "Don't bother those men down there and they won't bother you." She was right.

Far to the right of tin city was a pasture of rich land owned by the Honeleins, a German family. Their Hereford and Holstein-Friesian cattle grazed in this pasture. The Honeleins had a grocery store on the corner of Wheaton and Waters Avenue where they sold homemade cheese, buttermilk, hogshead cheese, liverwurst, bologna, and wieners. Our Aunt Emma was a nanny to second and third generations of the clan. Aunt Emma's son, Elijah "Tadpole" Green, worked for Honelien, but mostly Tad caddied at the Savannah Golf Club off Wheaton Street, where neither Honelein nor Tad were allowed to play golf. Before Tad left for Jersey City to work at Gillette Company, he began teaching our brother to play golf, and got him a caddie job at the club. He told James, "Learn the game, son, and one day you'll play on this course… you just wait."

Mr. Warren also took time with our brother showing him how to grow collards, watermelons, and sugar cane on his land across from tin city. Every year, he brought his mule, Bill, into a clearing near his house, hooked him to a contraption, and Bill walked lazily around a brick pit that had fire inside of it under a boiling pot. Mr. Warren pushed stalks of sugar cane into the bubbling pot and for weeks afterwards our street smelled of molasses. Mr. Warren sold his vegetables, watermelons, and dark syrup at the City Market in the Central of Georgia Railroad Station on West Broad Street. When he finished there, he rode on other streets singing, "Wallamelons, wallamelons red ta' de' rin three fa a Quarta, n one fa a dime…"

Elijah "Tadpole" Green

Fifth Street was more fun than watching our black and white television. Every one watched the children, and they told their parents if the children misbehaved. People spoke to one another up and down the street. They swept their steps and the ground in front of their houses, and the space under the stoop. They tended to patches of yellow marigolds, black-eyed Susans, and celosia plants called rooster cones.

On weekdays after homework, grownups sat out until sundown encouraging children to play fair.

"Ya'll oughta play by the rules and be good sports 'bout it, " they would yell from their porches. Sometimes adults played with us. Even Mom knew how to hit a baseball and run.

Frazier's Beauty Parlor was across the street from us. She made ZZZZZZZZZZ sounds in my hair. Smoke would rise from the side of my ears. I used to hold my ears down with both hands as her fiery comb straightened my hair.

In between appointments, Mom washed our hair and we plaited it or wore bouncy curls we made from rolling chunks of hair oiled with Dixie Peach onto twisted strips of brown paper.

"Tiggs, your girls keep their hair for a LONG time," Mrs. Frazier

Sarah

James

Emma, James, Marguerite

Emma

Marguerite

said. She was right, we did not want to go to that lady at all.

Mr. White owned the grocery store beside the beauty parlor. His house was actually on Sixth Street across from Mom's best friend, Lizzie Woods. Mr. White's backyard faced our street and 6:30 every morning we would see him swallow three or four turtle eggs and spit out the soft empty shells. Mr. White knew what we liked to buy, Mary Jane candy, popsicles, moon pies, pickled pig's feet, cold bottles of Sun Crush orange and Nehi grape sodas. He sold rickrack bollo bats, too, and never rushed us out of the store, even though we were in and out all during the day.

People on Fifth Street liked Mama, and we liked her too. We obeyed Mom out of love for her, and our fear of her. When she narrowed her right eye at one of us that was it. The rules and consequences in our house for misbehavior were very clear. Failure to obey meant a spanking with a rickrack paddle. After we did something wrong, Mom would say, "I'm going to give you a beating" (never on Sunday). Then, she would get the paddle from behind the trunk. When all of us were in trouble, we would wait our turn, and lay across the bed with our clothes on, and one at a time get a beating. We never understood that children could run from a beating. We never did.

Once, Sarah, Emma, and James did not get a beating, even when Mom discovered they found a bag of money and buried it in the backyard.

Mom said, "Each time I sent one of them to Susie Collin's store, or the China-man's, I noticed they had to go through the backyard first. By the time I found out, the bag of money was nearly empty."

"Y'all should be ashamed of yourself," she said to them.

This meant she was going to talk to them for a LONG time.

After having their conscience questioned for so long, I'm sure they felt limp as a rag, and wished for the beating instead. Whenever my siblings are asked, "How much money was in the bag," they answer, "A whole lot. It took a year for us to spend it."

Mom sighed, "As hard as times were, y'all buried the money - Lord Jesus."

She prayed often, but on Christmas, after all the gifts were opened, her prayer was short. When she said, "Now Lord..." we knew she was almost finished.

"Thank you Master for watching over us. Please keep us safe today. Amen."

We would kiss her, leaving with tangerines, bright colored candy, and Brazil nuts (Nigger toes) stuffed in our pockets. My sisters and brother went to skate under the subway, and I played with my things nearby.

Finally, one Christmas, Mom said, "Marguerite, you can skate in front of the icehouse, but don't leave Harmon and Gwinnett Streets." I was getting closer to the subway, and skating well enough not to embarrass Sarah, Emma, and James. I skated where she told me and stared in the faces of the Chinese children whose family store at the corner of Harmon and Gwinnett marked where I stopped. I wondered why they were not playing with their Christmas things, unless watching us have fun, was their fun.

Still, I wondered how they attended schools in Savannah that we could not. And, who is our father fighting overseas, anyway ?

Was it people like them?

And exactly where is overseas?

With my brown eyes, and their black ones, we looked at each other but kept our distance.

Little did I know, it was a rite of passage to roller-skate on Christmas under the railroad overpass. The steep hill started at the corner of Gwinnett and East Broad Streets, and the incline continued downward. Skating under the subway required speed, agility, and the ability to estimate distance. Master skaters liked Sarah's friend, James Frederick, showed their skills dressed in their new Christmas outfits. He would jump in the air, reverse his lanky airborne body, land on his feet, and while looking forward and skating backwards, he would make zigzag patterns on the pavement. He could stop on a dime, do a flourish, toss his long woolen scarf around his neck, and start all over again!
Nearly seventy other skaters did the same thing, going at least ten mph. This was a Christmas ritual.

In 1945, Daddy came home from Germany, where his all-Black Army regiment had fought against Japan.

Then, he left again.

Mama explained he was shell-shocked from the war.

We did not want her to cry anymore so we comforted her by saying, "He was sane enough to come home to see us, then he traveled all the way to Maryland and checked himself into a hospital. SHOOT!! Daddy will be home soon." But many Christmas' passed, and I became the only Tiggs still skating under the subway. Daddy continued writing from the veteran hospital in Perryville, Maryland, and we wrote him back.

Meanwhile, James and I attended Paulsen Elementary School

where Professor Robert W. Gadsen, Sr., was principal. He always wore a suit and tie. Later, Matella Maree became principal. She wore an armful of silver bracelets and when she stood in front of the school each morning, and rang the heavy hand bell "DEDUM! DEDUM! DEDUM! DUM! DUM!," those bracelets jangled. When the bell and bracelets stopped ringing, if students were not in class they were late, and had to go to her office.

Bertha Grissom taught me to read about Dick, Jane, Sally, and Spot in first grade. I felt really sorry for them because they never had fun like we did. Ms. Grissom looked as white as Dick and Jane did. Professor Gadsden's daughter, Lucy Solomon; Fannie Preston, Mildred Young, Retha Gibbs, and Augusta Petty were master teachers, who inspired us to always accomplish our best.

Back row left: Professor Robert W. Gadsen, Sr.
Mrs. Stegal installing Marguerite, Student Council President, Paulsen St.
School, Harmon St. Baptist Church, 11 years old, (1950)

19

After school, two or three times a week, I walked to Carnegie Library on Henry Street. Downstairs in the children's room, I would find Ms. Hatcher. She was fair and wore her mixed gray hair pulled into a knot at the back of her head. We sat on the cool tile floor in front of her as she read stories to us. Ms. Hatcher would show children where to find the most interesting books, and sometimes she would bring a book to me. It was as if she knew exactly what I liked to read.

We would also go upstairs to the adult level. There were stacks and stacks of books on shelves, and newspapers fastened over wooden rods. I often sat in a big chair in front of a large wooden table covered with beautiful brown skinned people in Ebony magazine. I used to stare through the window facing Henry Street into a small park with beautiful trees. The houses that were beyond the park looked like dream houses.

Mrs. Preston became my fifth grade teacher, and married Joseph Jenkins whom she called, Jenks. He came from Detroit to head the West Broad Street YMCA, where I went for Girl Scout meetings. One summer, Mrs. Jenkins arranged for me to be a mother's helper for her friends, the Greens, who had two children. Tecumseh Green was a coach at Claflin College in Orangeburg, South Carolina. In the afternoon, I walked Claflin's campus pushing the Greens' youngest child in her stroller, and walked close to their son. I already knew I would go to college and become a teacher one day.

Countess Cox, Georgia's first Black Girl Scout field director, taught seventh grade at Cuyler Junior High. Mrs. Cox's daughter, Antoinette, attended Paulsen where Mrs. Cox's mother, Clara Young, taught. Mrs. Cox came to our scout meetings. Once, she gave me a hand-me-down scout uniform. Antoinette's mother selected the uniform just for me because she knew I needed it. I wore it proudly, and when I recited the Girl Scout Oath I thought about Daddy in his Army uniform.

Mama worked in the school PTA. She sold her hand churned ice cream at the May Festival, and donated some of the money to the PTA. The Paulsen School May Festival was a big event. A king and queen were crowned and each grade performed for the royal court. The May Pole was exciting. We competed in plaiting streams of colored ribbons around a pole, skipping frantically to a recording of classical music played over the loud speaker. Boys were dressed in their white suits, and girls wore white organdy dresses with new Easter shoes.

"Don't put any Vaseline on those shoes until after the May Pole, or they'll be covered with sand," Mom warned me.

Eventually, we moved to Culver Street near our beloved church. Mom joined the Dura Deccas Social Club and entertained them when it was her turn. She taught me how to set the table, and where the salad and dinner forks were placed. She would take the set of silver (plated) from the trunk, and for days we polished it. Mom was a wonderful hostess. The Durra Deccas played pokeno and helped needy people at Thanksgiving. The only other time we used the silver was when our family had Thanksgiving dinner.

My friends and I often crossed Forsyth Park to get to Cuyler Street School on Anderson Street. We were Black so we could not play in the park, we could only walk cross it. Each morning Mom said, "Be careful." Arthur Dwight was our school principal, and he wore a suit and tie every day. The teachers I remember were Reverend Willie Gwyn, Ethel Luten, Katherine Manzo, and Virginia Kiah. Lasting friendships were made at Cuyler. Drucilla Moore was one of my friends, and Leroy Lockhart, Jr., was the first boy I ever kissed.

How could we know that Marguerite O'Brien, and Mozelle Collier, Dr. Henry Collier's wife, would become the advisors of The Jr. Debs, a club they helped us organize in order to further refine us. Mrs. Collier hosted parties for us and the boys we liked in their palatial Mills B. Lane home in Liberty City and at their beach house on Hilton Head Island. Only three other Black families had summer homes there, and there were no hotels on the entire beach . Under Mrs. Collier's gentle eyes we practiced social etiquette, and learned more about friendships and fun.
"When is our next meeting?" I asked Dru.
"We aren't meeting this week. Didn't you hear? The Debs are dancing in the Delta's Jabberwock, and Agatha Curley is meeting us at the Y to teach us a ballet routine to *Claire DeLune.*
"All twelve of us??"
"Yes."
We stuck together, and at Alfred E. Beach High School we were even closer. Otha Douglas was our principal. By then, we realized that principals and teachers dressed up each day to teach us.

Beach's home economics program included classes in observing children in the child development center and participating in activities with them. Betty Dowse, director of the center, impressed me in the ways she related to the four and five year olds in the center. This early exposure to the study of child development helped me to think of it as a career.

Back Row Left: Yvonne McGlockton, Gwendolyn Riggs, Margaret Solomon, Antoinette Cox, Gloria Mosley, Jo Ann Mitchell, Mary Carolyn Singleton Front Row Left: Emily Snype, Natilee Tucker, Drucilla Moore, Marguerite Tiggs, Purcell Grant

Each day for three years, after school, I changed into a white uniform and went to Dr. Phillip W. Cooper, Sr.'s dental office on West Broad Street. Everlethea Brisbane, one of Mom's friends, worked for Dr. Cooper, and when she left for the day, I answered the phone, made appointments for patients, and took payments. On Saturdays, Agatha Cooper usually brought two things for her husband; his lunch and their smiling four-year-old son, Wendell, to visit his father. Dr. Cooper beamed, "Hey Man."

Dr. Sidney Redden worked in the office and so did Julius Brantley, an honor student at Beach. Julius had excellent metallurgist skills that were put to use in the lab where inlays, and crowns were meticulously made. They would stop everything to talk to Wendell.

Wilhelmenia Dean was one of my teachers at Beach High, and a patient of Dr. Cooper's. Her husband, Elmer J. Dean was chairman of the social science department at Savannah State. When I entered college in August 1957, I got a work-study job with Dr. Dean. His office, on the second floor of Hill Hall, was next to a smaller office shared by the department's faculty consisting of Blanton Black, Joan Gordon, and Amjogollo Peacock. Several hours a day, I worked in this office typing and filing. Dr. Black and Dr. Gordon were as hilarious, as Mr. Peacock was humorless. I learned to work in the office and ignore their jokes, as Mr. Peacock did. Dr. Dean owned and raced trotters and pacers in Illinois, his home state and raced in Kentucky and Ohio. Dr. Dean's horse Kirk's Vote set a ten year winning record in Illinois. Dr. Dean taught Georgia History 300, a course we were required to pass before graduating. He often teased me, "Miss Marguerite, when are you taking History 300 ?"

Omega Psi Phi Fraternity
Marguerite seated second from right. Both ladies were guests of the fraternity.
Marguerite's mentors: Front row sixth from left, Dr Dean. Front row sixth from right, Dr. Cooper.

Eventually, the sit-ins started in Savannah. William K. Payne, Savannah State College president, was hung in effigy on the campus. It was said that President Payne disapproved of student involvement in some of the civil rights demonstrations in Savannah. I joined with students and went to prayer vigils, NAACP mass meetings, and sessions where we learned to carry picket signs and sit quietly at a lunch counter while whites – young and old, relieved themselves of their ignorance through filthy cursing. There were many brave leaders in the Savannah movement. I remember W.W. Law, mostly, because he was so focused. We felt braver and safer because he seemed and was fearless.

Grover Thornton, an Army veteran, and a political science major, was one of Savannah State's more vocal students. Grover talked about the non-violent beliefs of Martin Luther King, Jr., head of the Southern Christian Leadership Conference (SCLC), which was based in Atlanta. Grover knew that Walter Rauschenbusch's social philosophy principles influenced Dr. King, as did Gandhi's "Satyagraya." Grover's minister, Reverend Ralph Mark Gilbert, a civil rights activist, spoke from his First African Baptist Church pulpit about the work of Dr. King and the SCLC. Grover, and other students from SSC, including Drucilla and I, picketed in front of Kress on Broughton Street, and sat-in at Woolworth's lunch counter.

The sit-ins and picketing helped me realize that one can be afraid and still do brave things.

When Dr. King came to the Savannah City Auditorium to speak, Mama and I went together and listened as he talked about the power of love over hate.

Mom said, "You know what I hate the most? When your Father comes home, he may still have to sit in the back of the bus."

In my senior year I did student teaching in the first grade at Florence Street School. Norman B. Elmore was principal, and he wore tweed jackets and jaunty bow ties. He taught my sisters in high school, and asked about them my first day at Florence.

"Sarah's a nurse in North Carolina, and Emma's studying to become a nurse," I replied to Mr. Elmore.

Laura Martin was my cooperating teacher, and she said to me, "Now remember, when a child learns to read, it's like a light coming on in their little eyes."

During my practicum, when Mrs. Martin cleared her throat, I looked as she smiled, and winked at me...a child in the class was learning to read with understanding.

In June 1961, I received a Bachelor of Science degree in home economics with concentration in child development, and a minor in elementary education. My sisters of Delta Nu Chapter, Delta Sigma Theta Sorority, circled at commencement, and we vowed to keep in touch forever. Three weeks later, at twenty-two, I was at my first teaching job in a private day school in Newark, New Jersey. Tad was in Jersey City, and my brother James, a golfer, lived in New York.

After seventeen years…Daddy came home. He and Mom bought a house on Duffy Street, the street I liked to look at from the Carnegie Library's window. Daddy bought a Buick, and a Wurlitzer piano for Mom to take piano lessons… something she wanted to accomplish since her childhood. Daddy enrolled in a trade school and continued his leather crafting, some of which he sold. He joined St. Paul and became an usher. Mom continued singing in the senior choir and teaching the beginners class, as she had done for over twenty-five years. They traveled, went bowling, and played bingo at St. Pius. They went crabbing and fishing on Hilton Head, ate at Morrison's, went to wrestling matches at the Civic Center, and to baseball games at Grayson Stadium. They enjoyed being together. Our parents were like newlyweds!

Mom and Dad

25

In the summer of 1963, I married a Savannah schoolmate who moved to New Jersey two years before me. We made a good life together. We often visited his twin sister Bernice in Atlanta, and went to Pascal's, their first cousin's restaurant, where we enjoyed the Bird Cage, its well-known guests, and ate their famous fried chicken.

My husband and I were at work on November 22, 1963, when President John F. Kennedy was assassinated. During Thanksgiving dinner, we watched in horror as Jack Ruby killed Lee Harvey Oswald, Kennedy's alleged killer, right before our eyes, on national television.

Although I was unaware of the extent to which President Kennedy was hated, I was definitely aware of the racial tensions in Newark. Crime escalated, city services were declining, affluent and middle-class families of all races fled high tax yielding residential and commercial properties, causing many upscale shops to close; and once beautiful neighborhoods to be vacated. At the same time, Blacks were being excluded from high paying jobs in city administration, and in public education where they were academically better prepared than other racial groups who were disproportionately hired in the higher paying jobs. Teachers with a bachelor's degree from historically Black southern colleges were usually expected to complete additional education courses in New Jersey colleges to satisfy the state's teacher certification requirements. For years, this practice held many Black educators from tenure, salary increments, health benefits and promotions. For me, this meant attending evening classes after work at Newark State (Kean College, Union, N.J.). In two years I earned twelve credits, passed the National Teachers Exam, and received New Jersey certification as an elementary teacher (K-5) and certification as a home economics teacher. I had been teaching for nearly four years, and was now eligible for health benefits, and the first year toward tenure.

During this time, "The Dutch Man," a play written by Newark-born Imamu Baraka (Leroi Jones), was being performed off-Broadway. The scathing language in his work denounced institutionalized racial discrimination. Critics and theater audiences were divided in their opinions about Baraka, and his literary voice. Baraka led the Afro-American Liberation Movement, which signaled a new wave of social action. He and his followers supported the Newark rallies that raised awareness for Black economic and social empowerment. It was ironic at these rallies that many of us learned about the systemic differential practices, which compromised Black educators.

As Baraka saw it, Newark's children were hurt most of all. The movement established the Chad School, which was known for its family involvement, small class size, nontraditional Afrocentric curriculum, and well-schooled Black teachers. Chad was located on Clinton Avenue across from Father Divine's hotel on one corner, and St. Luke AME Church on the opposite corner, where Reverend Albert D. Tyson, Jr., pastored. My church Hopewell Baptist was a block away.

A sight to behold was seeing a cadre of teachers with a new generation of nearly fifty Black students, ranging from five years to twelve, each dressed in African attire, and walking down Clinton Avenue for recess in Lincoln Park.

Once, someone pointed to a Chad teacher who was dressed in a white galabao and matching headdress.

"That's Reverend Tyson's daughter, Margaret, do you know her?"

"No."

"He's the pastor of an AME Church...wonder how did she join Baraka?"

In 1966, tensions erupted in Newark. The burning of property, cowardice looting, shooting, and riots along the business strip of Springfield Avenue, and on Bergen Street, where I taught at Cleveland School, were violent and traumatic. Among the children I taught, many were displaced from their high-rise project apartments. Some grieved over a dead family member or friend. Others had relatives in hospitals or jails, or in both places. The horror of Newark's riots are as lasting as the killing of JFK.

On October 23, 1967, a day before my twenty-eighth birthday, Daddy died of a massive heart attack while sitting on his front porch. He was fifty-one years old. We told him countless times, "Daddy, we're proud of you."

Once, I said, "Daddy, even though you must have been so afraid when you were in the war, you still did brave things."

Our father was buried in Savannah's Oak Grove Cemetery. We watched the soldiers salute him at the graveside. A soldier played *Taps*, and another soldier folded the United States flag with graceful precision and presented it to Mama.

Daddy was twenty-six years old when he joined the service to better himself, and Mama was twenty-four. They had lived more than half of their young lives apart, yet, theirs was an enduring commitment.

Seven months later, another soldier died.

Martin Luther King, Jr., was assassinated, April 4, 1968, in Memphis, Tennessee. I cried, remembering 1966, in Washington, D.C., when I was in that crowd and heard him speak to 200,000 people about his dream. Now, two years later, Dr. King was gone. I feared what could happen next.

27

Another killing happened next.

Within two months, in June 1968, Robert F. Kennedy was assassinated as he campaigned at a California dinner for the Democratic Party's nomination to run for president of the United States.

All of the killings made me fearful. I knew I needed to recommit myself to enduring principles in order to ground myself.

When I learned that a contingent of New Jersey educators were traveling to the 1968 Poor People's Campaign in D.C., I paid for my seat on the Greyhound bus. Before his death, Dr. King was coordinating this campaign to focus national attention upon the plight of America's poor, including homeless and impoverished United States Korean and Vietnam veterans. While there, the New Jersey group, along with many others, built temporary wood framed houses, which showed how expediently the government, under President Lyndon B. Johnson's direction, could more efficiently do the same thing. The president needed to subsidize affordable low- income housing.

Reverend & Mrs. David Abernathy, Sr., arrived well dressed at the rain soaked federal grounds. Hundreds of people were already sleeping in make shift houses, tents, cars, trucks, and covered wagons. Reverend Abernathy spoke for nearly twenty minutes, and seemed uncomfortable with the SCLC mantle that was passed to him after Dr. King's death.

Someone whispered, "They didn't come dressed to build houses, did they?"

Later in the day, as food bags were distributed, some people grabbed the bags and pushed each other out of the lines. A Native American man from Lumbee, North Carolina, who was working up on a roof with us said, "This sure as hell ain't what Dr. King wanted."

We watched the ugly melee from the wooden rooftop and sensed that a dream was ending.

I did not know it then, but in three years my ten - year marriage would also end.

CHAPTER 3

I was divorced in July 1973, and Reverend Birt was divorced in May 1974. We met one Sunday, in 1974, and shortly thereafter, fell in love.

GETTING TO KNOW HIM

During our courtship Reverend Birt talked about growing up in Wrens, Georgia. The memories are easy for me to recall because he, his brother Garvin, and their sisters Beulah, Rosa, and Georgia Mae repeated them often enough at every family gathering.

This is what he told me:

I was the last of four children born October 3, 1918, to Luther and Amanda Jane Birt in Wrens, a rural town in Jefferson County, Georgia, about forty minutes from Augusta. Pa was twenty-eight and our mother was twenty-one when I was born. We grew up in an AME home. He was the Sunday School Superintendent for nearly thirty years. Our father had his own land and no one bothered him. Everyone knew "Mr. Luther Birt" had guns and would use them. He taught us how to shoot. Pa was the kindest man in the world unless you tried to harm him, then he could change on you. They called me Buster, but he called me Millard, and I wasted no time answering him, "Yes Sir." After our mother died, Pa married Falula Stapleton, a schoolteacher in Wrens.

We attended Spring Hill Grammar School and then Wrens High. I did well in math, world history, and geography. Can you believe I was a champion speller? Our teacher, Nellie Freeman, married Mr. Freeman, the undertaker. She weighed about ninety pounds and was four feet tall. We were big country kids and stood over her, but no one ever disrespected her. We read Erskin Caldwell's *Tobacco Road*. Caldwell had a home in Jefferson County. "Caldwell doesn't know a thing about the Black people he tried to write about," Mrs. Freeman often said. Instead, she had us reading and discussing Aristotle, Paul Lawrence Dunbar, Langston Hughes' *The Negro Speaks of Rivers*, The Book of Psalms, John Greenleaf Whittier, even *Bre'r Rabbit Tales*. She also taught us some Latin.

Back then, we didn't know it was called The Harlem Renaissance. We just knew people were going up north to New York and Chicago, writing poetry, singing, and show dancing... but we didn't

Standing: Amanda Jane Birt
Seated: Mother of Amanda Jane

know there was a name for it. I just wanted to go to FAR ROCKAWAY, NEW YORK to see what FAR ROCKAWAY looked like.

They used to say Garvin and me were Luther Birt's wild boys. The night Joe Louis knocked out Max Schmeling in 12.4 seconds - he beat that German, and everybody was on our front porch listening to our radio. It was 1938, everybody didn't have a radio. I could box pretty well myself. When I accepted the call to the ministry, lots of folk couldn't believe it was me. For one thing, when we got into Pa's model T Ford, with the running board on the sides, I'd drive down roads speeding like I was crazy, looking back to see how much dust I stirred up. Little children hollered,

Luther Birt , Brownie, Our Model-T Ford
(1949)

"WATCH OUT, HERE COME MILLABIRT!," and they'd run off the road. Girls in Jefferson County called me, THAT FOOL –DRIVING MILLARD..." they'd get off the road, too.

I preached my first sermon at Mt. Tabor AME Church, in Keysville, a town about fifteen minutes from Wrens. Folk came that night from all around, the church was too small to seat them. They were standing along the walls...and it was hot that night. People were looking through the windows from outside, just fanning. I was already bald, and the sweat was pouring out of my head, covering my face, all in my eyes, before I even started to preach. I had my sermon in front of me, and when I opened my mouth a different message came out.

My Pa knew I wanted to be a preacher.

"Millard, I'm gonna give you all the help I can, you just do your part. Don't just be a preacher, folk need to be ministered to. Don't fool yourself, there's a difference between the two..."

In 1942, The Women's Home and Foreign Missionary Society, under Lucy Hughes, gave money to help me go to Morris Brown College in Atlanta. Herman Rhodes and Julius Williams lived in Wrens...we grew up together and went off to the seminary the same time. World War II started...fellows we went to school with signed up for the service. We were all leaving...times were tight.

After I went to Morris Brown, I had to work in the summer to help pay for school. Once, a rich white man in Augusta hired me as a chauffer. All I had to do was drive his wife wherever she wanted to go. She had the cutest little show dog. One day, the dog was with me on the back porch with the leash fastened around one of the rails. The porch was high up off the ground and Candy was sitting there. I moved to the other side of the porch, and dozed off. Next thing I know the lady's screaming, "OH BIRTH!, BIRTH!" I jumped up and saw Candy hanging on the leash off the porch...dead. The lady fainted in front of me. I was sorry for dozing off, but shoot, you know I was fired.

We always owned a big dog, and after that, I knew I always would.

We graduated, in 1947, from Turner Seminary. When I went home to Wrens, I knew my Pa was proud of me because he took me in the bedroom and told me so.

Millard spoke reverently about his ministerial assignments. This is what he said to me...

Bishop William Alfred Fountain, forty-sixth Bishop of the AME Church, gave me my first appointment to Marietta Chapel in Marietta, Georgia. See here...Bishop Fountain wrote this introduction. Read what he said. (Millard showed me the *Encyclopedia of African Methodism*, a 688-page book written by Richard Robert Wright, Jr., and published in 1947.) In 1911, Richard Robert Wright, Jr., earned a Ph.D. in sociology from the University of Pennsylvania. He became the fifty-seventh Bishop in 1936. His father, Richard Wright, Sr., was the first president of the school you went to, Savannah State, back then, it was called Georgia State Industrial College. There's history in this book...people to be reckoned with.

He continued.

Later on, I was sent to Bethel in La Grange, Georgia and from there to St. Thomas in Claxton...you've heard about Claxton Fruit Cakes? They're made in Claxton, and they're the best.

Then I went to St. Paul's in Thompson. Have you heard of Paschal's Restaurant in Atlanta ?

I nodded, "yes," and decided to tell him later how I knew them.

The Paschals were my members at St. Paul long before those two brothers opened their restaurant. They started out selling fried chicken sandwiches.

I was doing all right, until an Ole Georgia Conference meeting. I had some words with presiding elder Barrow.

Mrs. Barrow said, "Reverend Birt, don't talk to my husband like that!"

"Tell him not to talk to me like that, Mrs. Barrow."

"You apologize to my wife for speaking to her in that tone, Reverend Birt."

He slapped me. Lord knows he was wrong to do that.

I balled up my fist and knocked him down flat. Right away blood shot from his mouth.

The Barrows WERE the Ole Georgia Conference.

I got out of Georgia FAST!

In 1952, I got a chance to see FAR ROCKAWAY, NEW YORK! I was in the First Episcopal District, and finally got assigned to Mt. Olive in Port Washington, Long Island. This was my first church in the north. By this time I was married and had a family.

Mt. Olive was a good church with some good hardworking members. We renovated the church, installed indoor plumbing and a new heating system. After three years there, I was transferred to the New England Conference and assigned to Grant AME in Boston. Pete Walker, Herman's older brother, was presiding elder in New England, and he helped me a whole lot.

Bishop George Baber was the sixty-third elected Bishop. In 1957, he appointed me presiding elder of the Brooklyn-Buffalo District. At thirty-three, I was the youngest to be a presiding elder in the New York Conference.

Standing: Reverend Birt Left: Cecelia Ann, Althea, Lewis, Luther

After serving five years, I returned to the pastorate and was assigned to Peoples Institutional Community Methodist Church in Brooklyn. This church split from Bridge Street AME in 1935. I was the second pastor in the history of People's, serving from 1959-1967. Peoples was brought back into the New York Conference and into the AME Connection incorporating the church as People's Institutional AME Church. Four hundred people joined the church while we were there, and the church burned a $101,000 mortgage. I'll show you my name on a bronze plate on the front of the church.

"That's an honor. I'd like to see People's one day," I said.

He continued...

I was transferred to the Philadelphia Conference in 1967 and assigned to Ward AME. Over 250 members were reclaimed. We burned a mortgage, installed folding doors in the sanctuary, and built up our Young People's Department (YPD). Now, that Selina King is some chorister, and Helen Jenkins is a master musician, too. We had GOOD SINGING at Ward! If you came after 10:45 in the morning, you sat where the ushers could put a chair.

While I was at Ward, I served under Governor Milton Shapp as chaplain of the Pennsylvania State Legislature in Harrisburg. I watched politicians cut throat with civility...it's an art! That's when I stopped smoking cigars and started smoking a pipe.

I traveled throughout the AME Connection. I've been to about every district. I've been an elected delegate to General Conferences since 1960, but there's ONE trip I'll never forget. It was a combination of the company I was with, and what we saw together. John D. Bright, Sr., seventy-ninth bishop, was Bishop in the First District at the time. I respected that man. He and his wife, Mrs. Vida (and their daughter) invited a group to travel abroad with them. There was Bill Freeman, James Dandridge, and his wife, Sister Octavia, the Connectional treasurer of the Women's Missionary Society; Richard Stokes, me, and a few others. Bishop Bright considered us his friends. Some people called us his henchmen. We visited Germany's West Bank and saw the Berlin Wall. We saw the changing of the Royal Guards at Buckingham Palace. We went to the Coliseum, to St. Peter's Square, and saw the Basillica, which is built upon Peter's Tomb. We were struck by the fact that the Vatican is a city governed by the Pope. But NOTHING compared to us walking the roads in Jerusalem where Jesus walked. When we stood on Golgatha's Hill, we knelt, and Bishop prayed. That is the trip of my life.

But my private life was another matter.

In 1972, Bishop Bright transferred me from Philadelphia to the New Jersey Conference and assigned me to Greater Mt. Teman in Elizabeth. It was not easy leaving my kids. The New Jersey Conference was led by a great pulpiteer- Larry Odum. He had a habit of wearing his clergy robe completely unzipped in and out of the pulpit... some of the brethren followed his style, but few could match Larry's political style. He was a BIG man, and when he wrapped his arm around you to talk politics, you couldn't move. I was going to take my time in Jersey... Jersey was not going to be easy either.

That summer, I went to the General Conference in '72, in Dallas, Texas, as a delegate from Philadelphia.

No AME will ever forget that Conference, even if you didn't go to it.

Richard Allen Hildebrand from Bridge Street in Brooklyn was elected the eighty-eighth Bishop of the Church.

Bishop Bright placed his Episcopal ring on Bishop Hildebrand's finger, sat in a chair, and died.

CHAPTER 4

Once Millard and I were married, we realized there was much to be learned, and most of it was not in a book...

LEARNING LESSONS

After a two-year courtship, Bishop Ernest Lawrence Hickman married Millard and me on Saturday, December 20, 1976 at Mt. Teman. Reverend O'Neil Mackey was best man, and Charlotte Gipson, was maid of honor. I became Mrs. Millard Birt, and moved into the two-storied eight-room parsonage beside the church. The next day was Sunday, and we were in church.

Our Wedding Day

Charlotte Gipson, Reverend O'Neil Mackey,Sr. Reverend Birt

Millard was *AME born and bred*, and I was Baptist. He became my primary mentor, guiding me as I read the Order of Service and other church rituals in the AME Hymnal. I read the *Discipline*, and marveled at a small gold bound *Discipline* printed in 1968.

"The AME *Discipline* is the first book of law published by Blacks in this country," he stated proudly.

At the time, Mary Frizzell was Connectional president of the Women's Missionary Society. My monthly missionary magazine, and the *Christian Recorder* newspaper kept me reading. Millard had a collection of journals from district conferences and churches where he formerly pastored.

His library was packed with Bibles, concordances, hymnals, and reference books with maps of the world. He owned a finely bound collection of literary classics. Over the years, he had added to his library, books written by his contemporaries including works authored by AME preachers that he knew.

"Here, read this."

He handed me pages of an unsigned letter with vile language that equally maligned Bishops, Connectional officers, and laymen of the church. The anonymous chain letter alleged financial mismanagement and graphic alleged infidelities practiced by individuals aspiring to Episcopal honors, and to Connectional offices.

"I've never mailed them on," he said, pointing to others neatly folded in his desk drawer.

"Here's a rule. The good thing is these letters only come out every four years before the meeting of the General Conference. True or not, the letters surface some of what people think. The bad thing is AMEs may forgive you, but they never forget.

I also started setting rules for myself.

On Saturday nights I stayed upstairs until he finished his sermon that he actually started on Wednesday. Afterwards, he would sit in his recliner in the living room with his sermon in his hands.

"Are you finished with your sermon?"

"I'm finished writing it on paper, but I never know what the Holy Spirit will do with it."

I learned that I needed the message just as he did, and just as the congregation needed it when the Holy Spirit got a whole of it. Therefore, I never wanted him to read his sermon to me before he preached it.

The New Brunswick Ministers' Wives and Widows' Alliance, met on the third Tuesday evening at a different church each month. I could not wait for the fellowship.

Reverend John Wesley Johnson was presiding elder of the New Brunswick district, and was known as Black Johnson to distinguish him from Reverend John Henry Johnson (secretary of the First Episcopal District), who was Yellow Johnson. No one called them by these colorful names to their faces. Catherine Johnson was our elder's wife, and met with us in our meetings. She was a veteran churchwoman with a cutting sense of humor. I learned there are unspoken rules for the minister's wife that are as important as those implied in the *Discipline*.

I suppose each minister's spouse observes and applies what they think is most useful to them. This is my shortened list:

Have my own personal relationship with God.
Pay my tithes and offerings to the church I attend.
I am a layperson and a spouse and not the pastor.
I don't have to be president of the local missionary society.
I don't have to be chairlady of Women's Day, every year.
I don't have to be at my church every Sunday.
I don't need to attend official board meetings, unless I have to. ,
Take care of the parsonage because it's our home.
When we have children, teach them manners.
Don't push for a seat at someone else's head table.
Don't let rude people be intimidating.
Wear gloves or wash my hands after greeting many people.
When we leave a parsonage, leave it in order.

Our friends were our teachers, too.

Reverend Arthur S. Jones (St. Marks, East Orange, N.J.) and his wife Erma frequently invited us to their Prospect Avenue apartment overlooking Newark's Branch Brook Park. Erma would cook in her small kitchen for twenty or more guests and turn it into an elegant banquet. We have been in their apartment when Bishops were guests, or Connectional and district officers of the church. We have been in their company when people of strong and opposing viewpoints were their guests. On each occasion, one could feel Arthur and Erma's warmth . Perhaps, the Jones' secret was to have people feel comfortable.

William (Nig) and Maxine Mathis lived in Kingston, New Jersey. Nig and Millard were schoolmates in Wrens, and kept their friendship over the years. Nig worked in ground security at Princeton University, and Maxine sang with the Sweet Adeline's, and was Kingston's fire commissioner. Nig had two adult daughters from an earlier marriage. Donna and Lloyd were Nig and Maxine's children. Maxine got along with Nig's older daughters, who dotted upon their younger stepsiblings. The laughter never seemed to stop. I wanted our home to be a happy place - especially for Millard's children. I determined they would have two homes to laugh in - one was going to be in Elizabeth with us.

Millard's friends, the Curtis Francis' (St. Paul, Pleasantville, New Jersey) became my friends. Millard and Reverend Francis made fun of Naomi and me to our faces. They teased us, and what is even funnier, Naomi and I laughed at us along with them. I learned not to take things too seriously.

It was not a laughing matter though, the year we went together to the Bishop's Council in Kingston, Jamaica. There were nearly sixty New York and New Jersey AMEs on the Air Jamaica flight. As we neared Montego Bay, the pilot announced "We will land in Montego Bay briefly for a health check. Please leave your belongings until you reboard the airplane." We deplaned reluctantly and went inside the terminal, while passports were checked.

Then someone yelled, "THEY'RE MOVING THE STEPS!"

Reverends Carl Hunter, John Ragin, and Floyd Black raced outside to the plane and wrestled the stairs from the men. They bolted up the stairs and banged on the closed door. By now, all of us were on the tarmac screaming in disbelief. We rushed inside the airplane and saw our seats occupied by white passengers.

"OH YES, YES, YOU ARE GETTING OFF AND YOU BETTER GET OFF NOW!" Elder William Lee Freeman demanded.

After we were airborne again, the flight attendants stayed in the cockpit with the pilots. They knew we were livid with anger. When the flight landed in Kingston, and we were getting off, some ministers stopped in the cockpit and questioned the pilots. One of them explained, "…We regret the inconvenience, but those passengers had waited all day for their flight. We were told to board them, fly to New York, and then come back for you."

"And what in the HELL were we supposed to do while the plane was gone to New York with all of our things," someone yelled.

"We need to sue you sonsabitches!!"

This was just the beginning.

When we arrived at the hotel, AMEs, young and old, were slumped in chairs and sofas throughout the lobby. We went to the check-in desk and heard the complaints. There was serious political unrest in Jamaica, and worse, there was a power outage. People had been waiting for hours to get into their prepaid rooms. There was no air conditioning, no elevator, or escalator service.

Millard took me aside, "Marguerite, you know I told you the American dollar was worth four Jamaican dollars...someone, somewhere, is making a financial killing." He went to the street with his American bills and came back loaded with Jamaican dollars. We had a hotel, too.

On our way to the hotel, the taxi driver said, "You'll be in the country, you'll like it."

After arriving, the hotel's brown-skinned owner greeted us at the front desk with a tongue in cheek expression, "Welcome, they did not consider our hotel for your Bishop's Council, in the least. The major white owned hotels are booked with your delegation, but not ours...thank you for coming."

"Well, we're here now, and there'll be more coming," Reverend Francis said.

The hotel was built in a circle. There were two floors so we did not need an elevator. From the inside looking up into the rounded skylight, we squinted our eyes from the sun shining onto crème-colored walls. As we walked in the round, we heard the most beautiful music. It was Leontyne Prices' recording of *Aida*, her voice reached the glass ceiling, and lifted our spirits.

Early next morning Millard pulled the sheers back from our ground floor window and looked in the face of a big cow.

"Well, I bedog, this is a HOOT."

He called on the phone, "Curtis, look out of your window."

After breakfast, the four of us played frisbee in front of the hotel.

"MD, MD, you're here too?"

"Yes, Man, and we're more than satisfied."

It was Reverend Joseph Joiner, the Secretary Treasure of the Pension Department and a former minister of Emanuel in New York City. Reverend Joiner and his new bride played frisbee with us, then we left for the sessions.

The Council lasted four days. On one of them, we hired a Mercedes taxi and went up into the Blue Mountains. Along the way, our husbands gave Jamaican dollars to children walking on the road neatly dressed in their school uniforms. The driver had rosin on his driving gloves so the wheel would not slip as he careened upward. We were high in the mountains when he pulled into a clearing and stopped.

"We not goin' anee farther up. Thos' housees way up thar in the mountains balon' to BIG People. Dey don' wan' ya' come anee closer. Dey already spot us, mahan. Dey see ya, but ya don' see dem. I always stop right har."

We headed down, and this time the closer we got to town, our husbands handed out American one-dollar bills.

On the fourth day, an earthquake frightened us. The rumble jolted the bed and woke us up. Reverend Francis was at our door.

"MD, let's get out of here!!"

After we got home, nothing more was said about Kingston.

"You mean nothing is going to be done about the airline putting us off the plane ?" I asked.

"Probably not. Jamaica is over and done with. The church is going on to the next thing," Millard answered.

Eventually, I took a leave of absence from teaching to be at home. In no time, we learned more about each other's routine. I was accustomed to getting up early and leaving for work by 7:00 a.m. He got up around 9:00 a.m., and made the bed the way his father taught him...the top sheet had to be the same length on both sides and pulled so tightly on the bed, he could bounce a quarter on it.

"Now, that's what sheets should look like. I don't care what you do, your feet won't get uncovered."

His suits were all neatly arranged on wooden hangers. His shirts were stacked in the chest by color in see-through plastic dry cleaning bags, ties on tie racks, and his shoes, with spit shines, were arranged on the closet floor. We both liked our clothing to be in order. It was the kitchen ritual that concerned me.

For breakfast, he would cook three cups of grits in three cups of buttered boiling water, eight strips of oven cooked bacon, six sausage patties, scrambled eggs with grated cheese, hot rolls, grape jelly, orange juice, his coffee and my tea. Between cooking and eating, he would have made and received dozens of phone calls, and sometimes company came over for breakfast (usually, Luther Miller).

Millard used big pots, big spoons and serving dishes. Although we had a dishwasher, he rarely used it. Instead, he ran hot water in the double sinks. In one of them he washed glasses, in the other, he washed dishes and silver by hand, taking them out with metal tongs and putting them in the other sink to rinse. He used tongs again to take them out as steam came from them.

"Who taught you how to wash dishes, Millard?"

"Our Pa. He told us that 'Nothing's clean, until it's as clean as you can get it."

I tried to do the dishes his way, but my hair would get puffy from the steam. Once, I was drying the dishes and put the dishtowel over my shoulder, he had a HISSY FIT!

"You don't need to dry the dishes, Marguerite, they're already dry, and don't put the cloth on your shoulder, then on clean dishes."

Lord help me if he had a morning commitment, and the kitchen was left for me to clean after he had cooked and eaten. It was a wreck!!

One thing his Pa did not teach him, and my Mom taught me was to clean up as I cooked. I knew that teaching school could drive me crazy too, but after five months at home I went back to my job to take my chances.

We learned that our routines clashed. He was a night person, and I was a morning person. Our most serious talks were late at night or early in the morning, and nothing in between. We were great compromisers and talked ourselves through disagreements. One of our settlements was he would wash dishes his way, and I would use the dishwasher. We agreed he would have his own checking account, and I would have mine. We would share expenses for major things, and SAVE OUR MONEY.

With one of our income tax refunds, we treated ourselves to San Diego, California, to visit Drucilla, my dietitian friend, and her daughters, twelve-year-old Angela, and ten-year-old Phyllis, who called us Aunt Marguerite, and Uncle Millard. After two days with them, we headed for La Jolla Beach in Dru's 18 foot Tioga-Arrow mobile home. Millard rode big-eyed in the front seat, looking through the wide window as Dru maneuvered the wheel on the fast moving expressway. The girls sat talking with me at the dinette table in the center of the room with two bunk beds neatly made. We hit the beach about noon, and went right into the ocean to swim. Behind sunglasses, I watched my husband frolic in the Pacific like a kid. Barefooted, he raced Angela and Phyllis down the beach and beat them twice.

"UNCLE MILLARD CAN RUN, FAST !," they said surprised.

We built a fire, like others along the beach, and heated dinner Girl Scout style in individual tin foil pouches on a rack over the flame. Dinner was sirloin steak, asparagus tips, baby onions, white corn, sweet potatoes with shaved orange rinds, and lemonade.

Dinner was not over, yet. He asked in disbelief, "We have WHAT for dessert?"

"Apple Brown Betty," Dru purred.

At sunset, we curled in blankets around the fire and listened to the breaking waves coming and going. I do not know what I was happiest about—seeing Millard in yellow Bermuda shorts and sandals, or knowing he was learning lessons too. There was nothing wrong with not wearing socks with sandals, and on vacation, he could miss a Sunday and not be in church. More importantly, he became a friend to my best friend!

In 1983, the Elizabeth Ministerial Alliance organized and elected Millard its first president. The members were Reverends Kenneth Grayson (Baptist), Jesse W. Mapson, Jr. (Baptist), William Hawkins (Presbyterian), and Elliot Cuff (Baptist). The alliance confronted Elizabeth's city leaders about employment, housing and education issues affecting African Americans and Latinos.

Simultaneously, Millard was elected chairman of the Board of Directors of the Elizabeth Neighborhood Development Corporation (ENDC). Federal and city funds were monitored by the board, which approved funds to contractors to rehabilitate condemned housing. The board monitored the sale of the renovated houses to low-income families. After a year on the board Millard noticed financial irregularities. His closest associates knew he could scan a financial report, and in seconds detect accounting errors. He could figure numbers in his head, and keep them there. He led the board in strategically questioning city administrators at closed meetings. This resulted in a changed climate between city hall, the ministerial alliance, the ENDC Board, and Millard.

In the midst of this, Reverend Martin Luther King, Sr., accepted the alliance's invitation to speak in Elizabeth at the birthday celebration of Dr. Martin Luther King, Jr.

Millard was beaming. "Daddy King's coming and Mt. Teman will host the program."

"Where is he staying?" I wanted to know.

"We got the news that Jimmy Carter's office is handling that, and also his transportation to Elizabeth from Massachusetts."

In a month the secret service had secured all of the telephones in the church and parsonage. Men with walkie-talkies stood on the roof of Nesbit's funeral home directly facing the church. On the day before the service, Reverend King's chauffeur called from the Connecticut Turnpike. The second call came when they crossed the George Washington Bridge. Each call was cleared by the secret service before Millard spoke to the driver. Finally, they were on Madison and East Grand, two minutes from the church.

The black limo gleamed. Dexter, Dr. & Mrs. King's second oldest child, accompanied Reverend King. The alliance met Daddy King in front of the church and shielded him lovingly. Madison Avenue was filling with people, some running to get a closer look at history. There were no cars on the street at all, except for the limo, and an Elizabeth police escort car. Up and down the street men were standing on the roofs of houses to the left and right of Mt. Teman -- guarding.

Reverend King was brought to the parsonage. After shaking my hand, he asked to use the telephone. Dexter placed the call and spoke quietly, then he passed the phone to his grandfather.

"Coretta…" he said.

Just as I went into the kitchen I heard Millard say, "I've got some chilled Georgia Elberta peaches…"

After eating them, Dexter untied his grandfather's shoelaces, lifted his stout legs, and turned him onto the sofa. He placed a pillow under his head. Minutes later, Daddy King was asleep on the sofa, Dexter asleep in a chair, and Millard asleep in his recliner. I quietly collected the empty bowls, and closed the front door to shut out the men watching from the rooftops. The next day, Daddy King preached to a full church. Before ending, he thanked God for his son…Dr. Martin Luther King, Jr.

At this time, Richard Allen Hildebrand was Bishop of the First Episcopal District. In the summer, the First District meets at Delaware State College in Dover for the four-day Educational Congress. Reverend & Mrs. Rudolph W. Coleman were associated with the college. Their church, Mt. Zion, hosted the Congress for years. Hundreds of AMEs attend the annual Congress that include classes for young people, sessions for missionaries, seminars for pastors, and a daily noonday worship, when everyone assembles. Reverend Floyd Flake (Allen AME, Jamaica, New York) became the director of the Congress with Bishop Hildebrand's blessings.

"That boy can PREACH!," Millard said.

As the Congress continued to meet in Dover during the summers, opportunities for life-long learning blossomed under the leadership of Reverend Flake and his team. After the birth of his youngest child, he carried a diaper bag with diapers, baby bottles, and toys over his shoulder like a Gucci. He could leave a room to change his boy's diaper out of sight somewhere, and return in minutes, not missing a beat. At that time, few ministers were manly enough to do this. It was a social and political statement to see his wife, Sister Elaine Flake walk into sessions with only her Congress bag over her shoulder. In truth, it was a timely statement between a husband and wife who publicly practiced, shared parenting.

When leaving Dover, it was a custom for AMEs to stop and buy fresh fruits and vegetables from roadside farmers along the way. We also made another stop. Either we arrived first at the Crab Shanty Restaurant or Reverend & Mrs. Herman Rhodes, or Reverend & Mrs. Richard Stokes. The first to arrive reserved the tables and got lobster bibs, claw crackers, picks, napkins, tabasco, and pitchers of water. When the six of

Greater Mt. Teman, Elizabeth, NJ

us were there, we ordered a seafood feast, and talked, until someone – usually, Sister Laura said, "We'd better get on up the road Richard ..."

Each time we parted knowing that some, who came into the Shanty, carried messages to others about "...Stokes, Rhodes and Birt being together." It was as if their being together was disloyal. Our husbands were aware of the political divisiveness the suspicions caused, still they kept their long, unbroken friendship, and watched.

"Learn to watch people," he told me.

He had a license to own a gun. I did not want him to carry it, and asked him why. He told me.

"Just keep it out of my sight," I told him.

Once after we returned from Dover, he went to use the upstairs bathroom that had a window attached to the roof of the front porch.

"CRACK!, CRACK!," shots rang from upstairs, then I heard a thud on the front and someone cursing.

"MILLARD!," I screamed.

He came down the stairs with the little silver revolver in his hand.

"What HAPPENED!"

"I was sitting there with the window opened, he put his foot through the curtain, and so I shot his foot."

"You shot the man ??"

"Yup, he came in on me. STUPID."

Mice also came inside of the parsonage. Once, I saw them come from between the pillows on the sofa where Daddy King had napped. I watched the two mice leaping and scurrying back and forth on the sofa. They were having a good time and I was sitting there looking at them, too mad to move. I did not know that mice leaped. To tell the truth, I

45

Reverend Martin Luther King, Sr. and Reverend Birt

think they saw me looking at them and just did not care. When I began to think that mice could have don't care attitudes, like the trustees who knew mice were in the parsonage, I was never the same. Millard was at a meeting in South Carolina when it happened. It was past two in the morning when I felt something run lightly across my chest. It was a mouse. I jumped out of bed and kept jumping and hitting myself to brush away, what had already gone. I was two months pregnant and wished for that silver gun.

I miscarried.

Before long, we moved into Mt. Teman's new parsonage – a red brick, nine-room house on a lovely street in Elizabeth's Elmora section. Millard, his son Lewis, and Hansome Ingram, a church officer, got on the roof of the old parsonage with sledgehammers and tore it down.

I drove over there during the month it took, to reprimand him.

"You shouldn't be up there tearing down that house, Millard. Let the church do it, it's their job."

He paid me no attention, and I understood why.

After the house came down, a mice bed was uncovered in the

46

backyard under Butch's doghouse. Butch was a terror of a German Shepard that belonged to the janitor's family who lived to the right of the parsonage in another house owned by the church.

When I looked into the hole, there were at least eight pink and squirming mice babies. The sight was sickening, even to Butch, who barked at them from the edge.

Mrs. Hogue brought out a pot of boiling water.

"Noooo, Mr. Hogue, I don't want to see you scald them to death."

"That's the only way to kill them Mrs. Birt."

I wanted those babies killed. I just did not need to watch it so I drove back to our new home.

"Millard, I will not live in another parsonage with mice."

Mt. Teman was going to host the New Jersey Annual Conference. As we prepared to entertain, an audit of ENDC began. By now, Millard had been given documentation of financial misdoings. Periodically, he met with a man who passed papers to him. The documents were under lock and key, Lord knows where. I became concerned for his safety.

"Millard, do you believe in the Irish Mafia?"

"YUP."

Sure enough, things began to happen.

After the old parsonage was torn down, the trustees planned to make a parking lot in the clearing to hold fifty cars. Verbal approval had been received from the city. Even the lady whose property would abut the lot, encouraged the officers. But the church received a restraining order instead.

I went to official board meeting.

"Reveren' we don't know what's happening. We have to stop. The lady also changed her mind... the headlights from the cars would disturb her. She's gone to Florida," Mr. Sykes said.

Albert Youngblood, another trustee, said, "We might as well forget the parking lot for conference."

Within days, Millard said, "Marguerite, we can't get a hotel for the missionary banquet."

"OH, LORD."

He reserved rooms in each of the hotels surrounding Elizabeth, but not one took the banquet. In desperation, a hotel behind the Newark Airport Cargo area was available. We feared for the safety of the people who were unfamiliar with the entangled 1 and 9 highway near the airport. A person could easily get in the wrong lane and end up at the tollbooth heading for New York City.

The night of the banquet, the waitresses wore jeans, and they

Inside: Reverend Millard D. Birt, Outside: Hansome Ingram

were rude. There was a water restriction in effect at the time. Tables asked for glasses of water, and were never served it. For most of the night Millard was following after the staff for service. The manager never appeared. Although Doris Garcia, the New Jersey Conference branch president, made kind remarks to Mt. Teman, we were embarrassed and angry. On Wednesday, the conference officially opened. Mayor Tom Dunn never appeared to welcome to Elizabeth , Bishop Hildebrand , his guests and the hundreds of New Jersey AMEs attending conference We knew then the extent of the mayor's disregard for Millard.

For days, I agonized over the conference knowing it provided fodder to those who regarded Millard as an outsider.

"This will pass," he said.

"Yes, but AMEs don't forget," I reminded him.

"And I don't intend to," he promised.

Weeks later, when the time came, he kept his word. The papers that were under lock and key surfaced. The Elizabeth Neighborhood Development Corporation had been shortchanged. The city received a slap on the wrist for its errors, and a low-level city hall accountant became the sacrificial lamb.

48

As the rancor became more legal, our baby daughter came into our lives at a perfect time, and helped us to focus on more precious things.

"Millard will you come home from the office before five, so I can mail some letters at the post office?"

"I'll be there."

After he came, I stuffed the letters into a canvas bag and hung it on the handlebars of the same bike I had taken to Jamaica, and sped off. When I managed to sit up, I knew I had been knocked unconscious. Blood was on my hands, shorts, and shirt. My legs were twisted under the wheel. The bag had gotten caught in the front wheel, and flipped me over, headfirst. I said, "Lord, have mercy," and my tongue went into a gapping space in the front of my mouth where my teeth had been – where were my teeth, and my top lip? "LORD HAVE MERCY." I dragged myself until I got to our house and entered quietly. I did not want Millard to see my mouth. He had to drive me to the hospital. Hurriedly, I packed ice cubes into a plastic bag and put it over my mouth, covering it with a red towel from the upstairs linen closet. I peeped into her room, and Amanda was sound asleep. He was asleep in the den downstairs. "Millard," I tried to say it softly, "I fell from my bike. Get me to the hospital."

He got the phone quickly, looking at me with the red towel over my mouth, "Mrs. Carolyn, my wife's hurt, come over with Amanda."

In the emergency room, the nurse removed the towel and Millard jerked backwards, moaning, "MY GOD!" I knew then, it was bad. A nurse took him out of the room, and I thought, "Big Baby!"

Hours later, the plastic surgeon said, "That was smart to put the ice on." He aimed a huge needle in my cheek and another needle deep, below my nose, and began to sew. Millard was right about his eye surgery. I was looking at the needle and thread going in and out of my lip, and I did not feel a thing. I went to sleep knowing that I would call my Mama, and she would come to see about her baby.

Within four days Mom came to help.

As my wounds healed, I had much time to think. I realized how quickly I could have been killed or paralyzed from the accident.

"Mom, I want to travel, and I need to do it now."

"Then do it."

She left the room, and went to join Millard in the den. My mind went over the summers he and I spent in Savannah.

CHAPTER 5

Mom took Millard under her wings and they became more than in-laws.

COME ON, SON!

After three weeks with us, Mom returned to Savannah.

"Millard, why don't you go to Savannah for the first part of your vacation?"

Later, that night I heard him on the phone.

"Mom, this is Millard, I thought about heading down your way for my vacation. You know Marguerite still has to stay out of the sun..."

The minute she hung up, I knew she would start spinning plans for him. She and Millard had memories of Augusta. She once lived there with Daddy after they got married, but only for a short time. Mom loved Savannah. She showed Millard the town introducing him to her favorite people, places and foods. She spoiled him with her crab casserole, deviled crabs, shrimp salad, collards, sweet potato pies, macaroni and cheese, white corn casserole, fried whitings, homemade ice cream, and hot pound cake. He never tasted frappe before she made it for him.

Mom introduced him to Savannah Mayor Floyd Adams, Jr.'s son and family who are her next-door neighbors, and to the Richard Washington's (he coached at Savannah State College, and she is my Delta sister) who live across the street. Helen Washington led her Duffy Street neighbors to preserve the integrity of the block. Mom was a member of the Dixon Park Association whose members fought against gentrification.

When we went to Savannah, Millard contacted friends like the Ben Gays from the Ole Georgia Conference whom he knew years ago. There was Reverend & Mrs. Charles Wells. He once conducted revival at St. Phillip Monumental when the Frank Maddox's were there. The Sunday he preached at St. Paul Baptist Church I saw Mom pointing to her watch to signal him they had a wrestling match to attend. I never had the nerve to signal him to rush a sermon. One summer Millard met Robert James, president of Savannah's Black-owned Carver State Bank, and he was more than impressed.

He often drove to Savannah without me, and loved the squares and the moss covered oak trees. He knew the riverfront and liked staying at The Mulberry, a luxury hotel, steeped in southern hospitality, across from the Savannah River. My sister, Emma, her children, and grands, got to know Millard better during his solo vacations. We knew how Mom liked picnics, beaches and boatrides. We had experienced Mom's expeditions to Derrick's Inn, Jekyle Island, Daufuski Island, and Fernindina Beach, Florida. She had worn me out years ago. When she latched onto Millard, she opened up a new world for him.

So many of the changes in the South that he lived to see gave him deep satisfaction. Blacks could sit anywhere on a bus. White men in Savannah opened doors for him, waving him in first. Wherever he wanted to spend his money, he could go through the front door to spend it. Once, he went to a Savannah Sand Gnats baseball game, and met the African-American woman who was a baseball club owner.

"I know my mother-in-law's friends," he bragged when he returned to Jersey.

There were the six wrestling buddies that included a man of Asian descent. They sat in the same section of the Savannah Civic Center eating peanuts and cheering for the same wrestlers. One of the regulars on the ticket was a wrestler of Asian descent, disliked by all six of them, even the man who was Japanese. "I went with them more than once" Millard said "and heard them yell at the wrestler from their seats, "...YOU DIRTY JAP!"

She had fishing and crabbing friends. One couple had a summer-house near the beach on Hilton Head. They would catch fish from a small bridge, and eat them for lunch on the couple's screened front porch, breathing the air off the Atlantic Ocean.

At one of our family reunions we compiled a journal called Special Memories. These are Millard's memories:

Millard's Memories

That night after he called, I knew he was thinking about being in Savannah.

"What did Mom say, Millard?"

"She said, COME ON SON!"

CHAPTER 6

If you can make it in New York, you can make it anywhere…

NEW YORK! NEW YORK!

I missed a semester at Rutgers after the bike accident, but my research continued. I discovered our society is a mobile one with few people still living in the same towns where they were born or reared as children. Business executives, military personnel, urban transients, migrant workers, and clergy members are among the most mobile groups in America. The transfer of ministers and their families from one church to another interested me.

When AME ministers move, there are support systems in place to smooth the family's transition. The quality of the support helps lessen feelings of discontinuity that is often experienced, especially by the minister's children and the wife.

Children may be at greater risk in their self-concept development and academic achievement when excessive movement occurs. Studies report that 5-6 year olds and teenagers are most vulnerable to the stresses associated with frequent relocations because the ties formed with friends are interrupted at a critical stage of emotional development. I believed whatever we learned during my research could be applied to my family since Millard would be moved at some point, and we had a child.

I observed the built-in support systems for the pastor include an immediate affiliation with the new church officers, and with the congregation. The pastor also becomes a member of the local, district, and conference levels…the connections are ongoing for an AME minister. The connections are also there for spouses who want to go with their partners.

HALLELUJAH, when the time came, I would be a trailing spouse and use the supports.

I watched carefully when I attended annual conferences. When AME ministers and laity stand at the closing service of conference to sing, *A Charge to Keep I Have*, it signals the presiding bishop's reading of his appointments for the new conference year. It is a time of recommitment to the service of God by ministers of the gospel, and by lay members.

Church law requires Bishops to notify ministers of an intent to transfer a pastor before the annual conference. Most ministers know if they are moving or staying, or to be assigned later. Nevertheless, the public reading of appointments is steeped in anxiety, politics, and AME traditions.

The reading of appointments is solemn, and each assignment is expected to reflect the bishop's Godly judgment. Who is sent and who remains are wrenching aspects of an annual conference. As the ministerial appointments are read, ministers experience emotions from anger and disappointment to outright joy. The minister's family sits planted waiting to hear the response from the audience that can range from groans to applause.

I will never forget the day, a senior minister of the church, dressed in his white suit, stood alone on the stage with a bishop waiting for his appointment to be read. There was silence. Then the bishop said, "…appointment to be made at a later date." The minister left the stage.

When we got home, I looked at Millard's appointment certificate and told him, "I'm proud of you." To myself, I thought, Lord, please do not ever let him be left on a stage waiting for an appointment.

The sermon about "Knowing When to Leave the Party" came to mind.

Months after conference passed, Mt. Teman's missionaries invited Yolanda King and Attalyah Shabazz to perform in Elizabeth. The daughters of the two martyrs , Dr. King and Malcolm X, had formed a company presenting monologues and music that focused upon self-pride, goal setting, and education. We had a sell out audience for the show. People came because of who their fathers were, and to see if they could perform. No one was disappointed, and afterwards, we served the tour company dinner at the parsonage.

Millard spoke to Ms. King, "Your grandfather was the speaker at the birthday celebration in Elizabeth of your father, Dr. Martin Luther King, Jr."

"Yes, I know," she said.

Then, it finally happened.

"Marguerite, would you like to go to New York?"

For the next five minutes, I bombarded him with questions.

"Remember Reverend John Brandon, he preached our last revival? We're going to his church in Harlem."

"WE'RE GOING TO HARLEM, MY BROTHER'S IN HARLEM!!" I screamed.

I would be in familiar surroundings. I studied for my master's at Columbia, went to the Apollo, and theaters on and off Broadway. I loved driving on the West Side Highway taking the curves as Jared did in Montego Bay; and riding the A train, going to the Metropolitan Museum, standing in line at Radio City for the Christmas and Easter shows with my brother's children Jacqueline, Christina, James and Stacey in tow.

Sure, I was ready to go to New York!

Bishop Frank Curtis Cummings, appointed Millard to Emanuel AME Church at 119th Street, on July 1, 1985.

Weeks later, the Bishop's wife, Martha Cummings, First District Episcopal Supervisor, called me on the phone.

"Mrs. Birt, this is Mrs. Cummings. I'm just calling to check on you and Amanda to see if everything is alright with you for moving to New York ?"

"I'm looking forward to moving to New York, Mrs. Cummings."

And that was the truth.

Catherine Johnson is a knowledgeable guidance counselor. She advised me to get a teaching job in a New Jersey town close to the New York line and commute to New Jersey. I had nearly fifteen years of New Jersey service, and did just as she said.

I was hired as a second grade teacher in Leonia, New Jersey.

"Squeeko," (Millard's nickname for Amanda) "we're going to move to New York. You're going to have a new house, a new school, and guess what... you're going to have a swimming pool."

Her two favorite things were swimming and Michael Jackson. She got down on the floor and did a break dance.

Millard watching Amanda in Holiday Inn pool, Henderson N.C.

"See, I told you, it's not bothering her."

Within weeks, her four-year-old mind realized we were actual leaving Grandmommie and PopPop Payne. His name was Jacob and h name was Jewel. The Payne's lived across the street from us and too care of Amanda while I worked and went to Rutgers. Their son Dell ai daughter-in-law, Carolyn, and their four children, lived next door to u The Payne's were like family.

Reverend Winton Hill, III was appointed to Mt. Teman. He ai his Bermudian wife, Damaris (herself a preacher's kid (PK)) had thr daughters. Lillie, their youngest, reminded me of Amanda when she w two. Mrs. Hill and I began to coordinate our moving plans.

From my studies, I knew that some children more than others a affected by the attitudes of their parents toward moving. If parents see anxious and bitter about moving, it is more likely their children will fe troubled. On the other hand, if the family plans the relocation togeth and talk openly about their feelings, children are less likely to repre their feelings. I was as happy about moving as Millard was, and hop for their children's sake, the Brandons and Hills were also happy.

We moved to 40 Holly Drive into the twelve- room Tudor-sty residence with an adjoining two-room apartment and bath. The propert valued at $300,000, is located in New Rochelle, Westchester Count New York, in what has been called the suburban bedroom of New Yo City. The centerpiece is a ten feet deep, seventy-five feet long heated, i ground swimming pool. The property was purchased during the pa torate of Reverend Grant Grady Crumpley. He and his wife had twel' children (sets of twins).

That Saturday, as we finished moving in, Reverend & Mi Robert Brown, Jr., of Greater Bethel on 123rd Street were our first vi tors. They brought their granddaughter Tehera to meet Amanda.

"Amanda, you and Tehera are going to be best friends, we can te the way you're smiling at each other."

"Thank you Jesus for this new AME friend for Amanda," I pray silently.

The Browns lived fifteen minutes away in Mt. Vernon. I was do bly happy at the prospect of our friendship with them.

The next morning Millard left for Sunday School.

"We'll be there before eleven," I said.

Then, Amanda and I left for church. It had not occurred to me get directions from New Rochelle to Emanuel. I only knew how to g from Elizabeth to New Rochelle, not from New Rochelle to Emanuel was hopelessly lost in Yonkers.

By the time we reached the church, Millard was ending his sermon.

After he sat, Willie Lee Crumpley, Reverend Crumpley's widow, repeated the welcome to Amanda and me, and pinned us both with flowers. Mrs. Crumpley was known for her radiant smile, elegant clothes, and designer hats. Emanuel loved Lee Crumpley, and before long, I knew why.

Following service, the church photographer, J. B. Scott, and his wife, Miriam (herself from Wrens, and Reverend Julius Williams' sister) took us to dinner. Not one officer mentioned a meal, or offered money for us to buy one.

I trailed Millard back to New Rochelle feeling uncomfortable with our welcome.

"This is my first move. What if the people don't want us here."

Millard spoke gently to me, "Marguerite, I have pastored churches where some members wanted the pastor to leave, and some didn't want me to come. But that's not the point. My job is to be the pastor, and minister to them, as God would have me do. When the time comes for me to leave here, some of these people will want me to stay, and some will want a new pastor to come. That's the AME church. But for now, we're here and we'll be fine."

Early Monday morning, Mrs. Kitt, who was president of the pastor's aide, called.

"This is Mary Kitt, and if there's anything...I mean ANYTHING we can do for you, just let us know."

And we did.

In two days, Mary Kitt, Pearl Chambers, Marilee Leacock, Florence Glover and Evelyn Sumter came to the parsonage and worked all day in it.

There were badly needed repairs. The ceiling leak in Millard's first floor study was the worse.

"No, Marguerite the uncovered gas pipe on the patio of the pool is the worst," Millard said. "They had a gas grill out here, and disconnected the lines ... and just left it."

"Mrs. Kitt, where are the curtains? I've counted twenty-five windows so far."

Then, the non-English speaking gardener came by the next week.

" No, speak English. You pay me please Reverend Dirt?"

"We'll see that you get paid Sir. But, let me get an understanding about what you do here and how much it costs the church."

Several weeks passed by now and the church had not paid Reverend Dirt either.

After two months, and still no salary, Millard paid the gardener with his money because our neighbors, the Leon Wrights, warned us that snakes hide in Pakistani plants, and that's what bordered the front lawn.

One day, I closed myself in the guest bathroom and looked around me at the expensive wallpaper, a small crystal chandelier with teardrops hung from the ceiling over a corian top sink. The water fixtures were two golden faucets shaped like birds' heads. The crème-colored vanity edged in gold filigree matched the corian sink. No matter how hard I tried, the window in the bathroom that faced the street was off the track and would not close shut. There was much work for us to do in the parsonage.

Emanuel is the third leading church on the Manhattan South District. It sits between brownstone apartment buildings on 119th Street between Lenox and Madison Avenues. The church's gothic architecture replicates the Notre Dame de Chartes in Chartres, France. Its luminescent stained glass windows add to its splendor. The sanctuary has high ceilings and a seating capacity of over 2,000. When Emanuel's master musicians, Coris Murdock and Evalethia Williams, play the Wick organ, and the combined choirs sing the great anthems of the church, it is, they say, "HIGH CHURCH."

Most of Emanuel's members have roots in South Carolina, with second, third, and fourth generations of family members in the congregation. Many of them travel great distances to the church by subway, buses, automobiles, or in private cabs that New Yorkers call cars. Some members pass other AME churches on their way to Emanuel.

The Dalton Greens come from Newark, New Jersey, nearly an hour's drive. They are Sunday School Bible Class teachers and arrive by 9:30. Mrs. Green's mother was a faithful member at Emanuel. This is true for many members – they come because of a family legacy.

Edward Brown, chairman of the trustees and president of the New York Lay Organization knew Emanuel well.

"Emanuel AME is a proud church...we have a right to be. We have had great pastors. In 1940, Decatur Ward Nichols was elected the fifty-ninth Bishop from Emanuel."

"They know that, Brother Brown. They know he's from SOUS CALINA, too!" Mrs. Kitt added.

"You, from Calina too, Mary Kitt."

"You too, Brother Brown."

119th Street, is filled with brownstones.

People sat in their apartment windows, along 119th Street and those nearer, began calling us when we drove up to church.

"Mo'nin, Revin Birt!!"

"Mo'nin Miss Birt!!"

They also began speaking to Amanda.

Tightlipped, she asked, "Who's that calling my name?"

"We don't know yet, just speak back," I answered.

"No, they're strangers."

I tried explaining knowing that people are quick to say minister's children do not speak to adults properly. "Well, we don't know everyone yet, just speak."

Out of her hearing, Millard said, "They are strangers, leave her alone."

Reverend Willie Lee Freeman was Millard's new presiding elder and no stranger to us.

"Bill Freeman is one of the most powerful men in the AME

church. Every Bishop takes Bill Freeman serious, especially when it's time for them to move. He's not vice chairman of the Episcopal Committee for nothing."

Reverend O'Neil Mackey, and his wife, Gloria, whom Millard called, Glory Hallelujah were no strangers either. They were at Bethel on 132nd Street, the first leading church and only thirteen blocks from us. The Frank Emmanuel's were at St. Luke, the second church on the district.

The Mackey's identical twin daughters, Karen and Sharon called Millard, "Birt." They had a ritual between them. Millard would say, "I use to change their diapers" and they would just smile.

The diapering had actually happened when Birt and their father pastored in the Philadelphia conference, over twenty years ago.

I met O'Neil, Jr., the Mackey's teenage son, who was an active YPD member. Again, I prayed silently, "Thank you Lord, he can be a big brother to Amanda."

Our support system was growing. I imagined how the swimming pool and Westchester house could be a gathering place for family and friends.

"That kid swims like a fish," Millard remarked as we sat around the pool watching her climb onto and walk the thirty-six feet diving board, and jump in. She would come up smiling with her eyes wide open. Amanda had no fear of the water, so we enrolled her in a class for beginning swimmers for her to learn about the dangers of water.

Since neither of us could swim like our daughter, we bought a life preserver and showed her how to toss it into the pool in case one of us needed it.

When it was time to return to school, Amanda went to kindergarten at a school right behind the house. We hired a lady to stay during the week, so that someone was always in the house when she came home from school.

I drove to Leonia, a small middle-class town, just off the George Washington Bridge. The commute was less than forty minutes when the traffic was moving. There were 279 children in the school, and as far as I could tell there were three African-Americans…two students and me. I had fifteen eager, and self-disciplined white children in my class. Their parents were quick to volunteer in the classroom and watched me carefully. We all benefitted.

Catherine's advice was perfect. I did not have to give up my New Jersey tenure to trail my husband.

As the months passed, Millard warned me, "You're going to need a heavier car when it snows. That George Washington Bridge is nothing to fool with."

I listened to him and for my forty-sixth birthday, on October twenty-fourth, I bought myself a smoke gray, 1985, four door Lincoln Towne car, and named her Josephine.

When winter came, I left home and returned in darkness. At times, when I drove over the George Washington Bridge, winds that were caught in the chasm between the New Jersey palisades and New York's Hudson River pulled at my car. But, Josephine held steady, as Lincoln's do.

On the days that I drove from work to my classes at Rutgers in New Brunswick, my commute was nearly two hours. I would get to New Rochelle after eleven at night. I began listening to Family Radio and never turned from that station. During those long rides from Jersey to New Rochelle, I was immersed in the broadcast sermons, Bible discussions, and prayer. I would hear old hymns. Sometimes, tears filled my eyes as I listened. My relationship with God grew stronger while driving on the New Jersey Turnpike. I began to realize more deeply that I was in a joint ministry with Millard. The realization was bringing me closer to God and closer to the man I married.

One day, snow quietly covered Leonia so quickly, by the time school was closed, the town's slippery hills were inescapable. It was impossible to reach any entrance road to the highway. After an hour of going around in circles, I drove away from Leonia to a plush hotel in Rutherford, near the Giant's Stadium and called home.

"Millard, I can't get to the bridge."

"And you can't get into New Rochelle either. Cross County, Bruckner, and some of 95 are closed. Mrs. Brown is looking after Amanda. You want to speak to her? Do you have gas in the car?"

"Yes," I said to both questions.

The needle was near empty when I got to the hotel, so I lied.

That night I prayed, "Lord, please help me get a job closer to home."

As time passed, Millard faithfully held board meeting on Monday night, Bible study on Wednesday night, love feast before first Sunday Communion. He was an instructor in the ministerial institute, member of the Board of Examiners, and member of the finance committee for the First District. He attended meetings of the William Lee Freeman Scholarship Committee, and contributed substantially to its funds. He was a member of the New York Ministerial Alliance, the 119th Street Block Association, and a life member of the New York Branch of the

NAACP. Millard was presented with the Morris Brown New York Alumnae Chapter "Man of the Year" award. In ten months God answered my prayers. I began teaching in New Rochelle, less than ten minutes from home.

On an autumn day, in 1986, Bishop Cummings officiated at the mortgage burning ceremony of the parsonage on the front lawn of the house. Nearly one hundred church members and friends attended. Refreshments were served. Mrs. Crumpley and I co-hosted, and directed the tour. Lula Williams sat with the guest book at the front foyer in one of her wide brimmed fashionable hats. We wanted to remember the occasion...some members had never seen the parsonage, let alone come inside of it. And it is THEIR property. However, the gas pipe near the pool was still uncovered.

Burning the Parsonage Mortgage (1986) Bishop Frank C. Cummings, Althea, Elder Willie Lee Freeman, Reverend Birt, Marguerite, Amanda

Finally, in 1988, after over four years in graduate school, part-time, I received my doctorate in early childhood education. My dissertation was titled - The Effects of Transciency Upon the Academic Achievement of Urban Elementary School Pupils. I kept an interest in this topic for forty years ever since the summer, in 1958, when I went to King Ferry and worked with migrant children.

Within months, I was appointed assistant professor of early childhood education at Farmingdale College of Technology on Long Island. To reach the campus, I passed Port Washington, the first town in the north where Millard pastored. Less than three months later, I accepted an adjunct position at Queens College in Flushing, New York, to teach in the home economics department the course, Marriage and Family Relations, and another course, Contemporary Family Life.

God was blessing us abundantly.

"Marguerite, Emanuel will host the New York Annual Conference," Millard beamed. Although it was more than a year away, it was not too early to prepare for it.

"You won't believe this, we went to the bank today and they turned us down for a loan. Fifteen minutes later, a man who says he can help calls me at the church. He's coming here tomorrow, and I want you home to hear this…"

The man came to the parsonage. I heard Millard say, "You've made quite an offer, it's just not the way the church wants to handle this."

"You can keep us in mind, Reverend, you never know what might happen."

He looked Italian. I gave him his cinnamon colored cashmere coat as he prepared to leave, and admired the thin-soled leather shoes as he walked away.

"That's the Mafia, we're looking at Marguerite, and he's working with the bank. We're not crazy enough to get into that…We're going to find a legitimate bank. After all, the church has assets, and we're paying our bills on time. We're going to find a bank to do business with Emanuel. I wish Carver State Bank was up here…"

Eventually, a plan was made. Church officers and members who could afford to lend their personal money, and wait to be repaid, after a bank loan came through, would donate funds to Emanuel.

Millard led the way by lending several thousand dollars to the church from his savings.

"This isn't anything new we're doing. Don't you remember that our founders believed in self-help? The AME Church is built on self-help."

Others remembered, especially Evelyn Sumter who immediately followed Millard with her loan … then a few more, more and more.

When Bishop Cummings opened the 167th Session of the New York Annual Conference on April 24, 1989, Emanuel was ready, THANK GOD!

The worship services, the reports, and the work sessions were all spirit-filled. The Wick organ had been precisely tuned, and the conference choir, sang the songs of Zion!

To eliminate the travel to New Rochelle, as a courtesy, Reverend & Mrs. Frederick G. Harrison (Executive Secretary/Treasurer of the Connectional Missions Department) permitted Emanuel to serve meals to Bishop & Mrs. Cummings, and their guests at the newly renovated AME mission house, a handsome three-storied brownstone on 135th Street. Mary Kitt was in charge of the meal service.

As the conference was ending, the young woman who promised

to stop the conference, until her charges against a minister were heard by the Bishop, attempted to keep her word. After service, we went to the mission house and waited over an hour to serve lunch.

Finally, Millard called, "We wait…Bishop is handling some business and we wait."

Bishop Decatur Ward Nichols and one of his daughters were at the mission house, and graciously declined to be served until the Cummings arrived. How does one not feed the senior Bishop of the AME church! He brought the people into Emanuel church in the first place in 1920, he had the majestic Wick organ installed there, and he was patiently resting in a chair.

"Mrs. Kitt, my husband said 'wait,' and we're going to follow orders. I know it's uncomfortable, but it will be alright."

Another hour later, Mrs. Kitt put her hands on her hips and stood beside Bishop Nichols. She spoke softly to him, "Now Bishop Nichols, this don't make no sense, I'm gonna feed you… you git up and come to this table, and eat this food. This ole lady from Sous Calina, mean every last word."

Bishop Nichols and his daughter sat alone and dined sufficiently.

Mary Kitt was right… this is just what Bishop & Mrs. Cummings wanted us to do.

CHAPTER 7

I wanted to travel and see what *overseas* looked like.

TO SEE FOR MYSELF

Three months later, I was riding upon a slobber mouthed, sure-footed dromedary camel near the Sphinx in Giza, Egypt. I was keeping my promise to travel… "to just do it," as Mom said.

Cairo, Egypt. Marguerite in the middle

I was among one hundred twenty other American professionals attending the Fifteenth Annual International Conference of the National Association of Black Social Workers. The fourteen-day itinerary included seminars and tours throughout Cairo, and surrounding regions of Egypt.

Dr. Wynetta Frazier, (University of Illinois) and I were co-presenters. Her research related to the increase mortality rate of African-American infants, and my paper was about the effects of transiciency upon self- concept development (same interest!). E. Hill DeLoney, (NABSW) executive director commented, "...the topic of childhood development is relevant anywhere any time, but it is of particular interest as we visit our Nubian family in Africa. The bridge between our family here, and in Africa, in developing our children, should be emphasized in how we, as African-Americans, can help provide assistance, even if an ocean separates us."

I went to present my paper, and to experience Egypt. I would see the six pyramids that took slaves, engineers, and artisans hundreds of years to build. I would see for myself that the broad, flared nostrils, and portions of the ears have been selectively removed from the Sphinx. I would climb each step inside the pyramid of Khafri and enter chambers, in countless rooms, to view a people's history etched on walls in hieroglyphics. On the wall of one of them was a *birthing table* precisely slanted with a hole in it. Below it was a waiting basin for the newborn. I would see the obelisk that was perfectly carved from a single flawless piece of limestone bedrock taken from the earth, and ride on the Nile in a felucca. I would see Nubian men walking past with their pinkies locked together, and perhaps glimpse a Nubian sister's veiled smile. Seeing all of this would last me for a lifetime.

Yosef Ben-Jochannan, the renowned Egyptologist, accompanied some of the tours and gave his commentary. After dinner, we gathered in the hotel lobby, and he led discussions. The day we went to the Cairo Museum the guide was a white Egyptian lady. She and Dr. Ben were having words even as we boarded the bus. At one point during the tour he asked her, "When are you taking them to the lower level ?" She answered loudly, "Keep away from me!" We understood then he wanted us to go downstairs, and she didn't.

Someone yelled, "Everyone coming with Dr. Ben follow him!" The lady was angry as she headed toward the entrance doors. We turned to follow Dr. Ben walking briskly down the spiraling granite stairs until he reached the bottom. Once there, he opened his arms and said, "This is what you wouldn't have seen."

UNBELIEVABLE... the artifacts were crowded and in disarray everywhere! The sights were in muted shades, and seemed surreal. As we walked through the rooms we saw the creations of the ancient Nubians- the possessions they wanted with them in the afterlife. There were magnificent tapestries, opulent rugs made from skins of panthers and greyhounds, papyrus scrolls, exquisite eating utensils, pottery, and bowls of every size edged in gold. There was jewelry adorned with garnet, turquoise, honey-colored amber, and the deep blue lapis lazuli stones. In one room there stood an enormous horse carved from cedar trees that seemed higher than three 6 feet tall men. We saw carvings of game boards, and statues of domesticated and dionized dogs, cats, hippos, birds, harps, walking sticks, and throw sticks to kill birds and fish. The Nubians buried with them their beds, couches, headrests, footstools, chests and assorted furnishings. In other spaces we saw carpentry tools, models of boats, called dhows, these too, were intended for the afterlife. Weaponry filled the walls - bows and arrows made from reed and tipped with flint, daggers, battleaxes, spears, bronze shields, and knives. There were canopic jars, amulets for holding death portions around the neck, embalming tools, slate palettes for mixing eye paint, cosmetic spoons, hair ornaments, combs of ivory made from elephant's tusks, or from the hippo's teeth, and fly whisks from the giraffe's tail that denoted wealth.

Dr. Ben guided us and gave details about what we saw with authority. Some, lingered behind, and some wept. The lower level of the Cairo Museum that day was an emotional unveiling. Forgetting time, we had overstayed ourselves in the basement. With Dr. Ben still leading, we reached the main floor, and saw guards standing inside of the doors. As we approached, they unlocked the doors for us to pass through. Then, we saw the four guards bend their heads in homage to him, and said, "Goodnight, Dr. Ben." We could tell this had happened before.

That night we met in the Oberi Hotel lobby relieved that Dr. Ben was not present to hear our anger toward the lady guide. She represented a system that would deny knowledge of our connection to Egypt's earli-

Dr. Josef Ben-Jochanna Cairo, Egypt

est people. How dare she decide what we could and could not see? A more troublesome question is how many others had she misguided? At the close of the conference we vowed to be more careful of whom we permitted to lead us...who we would follow in our personal and professional lives.

After returning home, nearly three months later, the woman who delayed the New York Annual Conference, while she accused a minister of committing adultery with her, was instantly killed when the car in which she was a backseat passenger was struck from the rear by another car. The news of her tragic death left many people saddened and speechless. AMEs are not speechless for long because the work of the church goes on.

I became aware of the commitment to the work of the church going on during my tenure (1991-1994) as second vice president of the New York Conference Branch Women's Missionary Society (Thanks Flora Eastman for mentoring me.). Carolyn Scavella was president, and Margaret Bell, first vice president. These sisters are prayer warriors! Carolyn is a strategist, with the heart of an angel . Under her leadership unique missionary programming emerged such as the Conference Founder's Day Red and White Luncheon .

In the journal, Carolyn wrote: "...This book is an attempt to document some of the talents and achievements of first ladies of the New York Conference, in and outside of the church. We thought, who knows them best? Who could write the real story?...why their husbands of course...the pastors of the New York Conference."

This is what my husband wrote:

One Sunday morning in Greater Mt.Teman AME Church in Elizabeth, New Jersey, I made an announcement asking if there were any persons present holding a master's degree in early childhood education to please meet with me in my office after the benediction, among the persons that came was Marguerite. So, I told them of my intentions to open a Head Start program in the other wing of the church and that I need someone with a master's to proceed. They all wished me well, but Marguerite finally said that it may be possible for me to use a copy of her early childhood certification. I was very pleased, and asked if I could have her phone number and that sometime during the week I would call her to further discuss what we would do. I did make the call, and during our many conversations I discovered that we were somewhat attracted to each other. After two years and eleven months, she became my wife. Marguerite is a very determined person and one must be very persuasive to deter her from any goal she has set for herself. She is very adamant in her ideas and has a hunger and thirst for knowledge. Marguerite is a born teacher, enjoys imparting her knowledge to others, whether they are children or adults. She loves her family, friends, church and God. She is a much-loved companion, and we wish for her the best that life affords.

This is my love letter from him.

The responsibilities of the second vice include working with the fourteen standing committees of the conference. In this capacity, I gained more respect for the organized work that is done in committee. The standing committees in the AME Missionary Society at the local, conference, district and connectional levels facilitate the service given to others by missionaries.

I have the perfect example of extraordinary committee work.

Bishop & Mrs. Cummings visited Zwide Township in Port Elizabeth, South Africa. Zwide is located on the coast at the southern most tip of South Africa. Most of the men leave the township to work in the city in automobile construction, the country's leading export industry. Women work on out-lying farms away from their homes and children for long periods of time. Although grandparents in the villages look after the children, the daycare center filled a need, but it was now run-down and closed. A hat was passed among the United States delegation and money was given to start a fund to rebuild the center. Mrs. Cummings supervised committees of missionaries in the First Episcopal District that partnered with committees in South Africa's Eighteenth Episcopal

District, presided over by Bishop Robert Thomas, Jr., and supervised by his wife Mrs. Beverly Thomas.

Wimphrey Jenkins of the New Jersey Conference was coordinator of the First District's efforts. I served on the committee and designed a model curriculum for the center.transcontinental collaboration occurred over months between the two supervisors. Frequent phone conferences and faxes were the means of communication between committee members. A walk-a-thon was held at the Educational Congress in Dover, Delaware, and over $24,000 was raised and delivered to the South Africa project. Mrs. Thomas, an accomplished artist, donated money to fundraising from the sale of several pieces of her artwork. The committee work was a global collaborative.

Months before my scheduled surgery, I called Wimphrey.

"I have mailed the Birt-Educare Curriculum to you for the committee to review. I'll be unable to work on the committee for a while."

"Thanks for what you've done, Marguerite. You think about getting better. You know the work will go on..."

Months later, on November 20, 1991, the Martha C. Cummings Child Development Center in South Africa was renovated, refurbished, reestablished, and REOPENED.

That autumn, while recuperating, I looked out the second floor bedroom window in the direction of the maple tree on the left side of the front lawn, where strange roaring sounds were coming. It was a sunny day without the slightest breeze in the air. Then, there was a surge of wind. The giant tree was pulled out of the ground by an unseen force so powerful the connecting roots clung pitifully to the soil and shook grotesquely as it was finally separated from the earth's bed. For seconds the wind ruled that massive tree by tilting it to the right and slowly laying the trunk across our front yard. The branches were covered with amber and red leaves, and filled the street without touching one neighbor's house.

I had just witnessed God's mighty power, and now there was only silence. Maya Angelou's poem, *When a Tree Falls*, crossed my mind. I got my pen and journal to write my own thoughts:

Stillness
Stillness, silence is near,
Touching deeply within,
Restraining, rejoicing, renewing.
Silence is stillness.
Wait, a new strength is near,

Where is its mind...in a peaceful heart?
Waiting is stillness
Listen, a new understanding is near.
Words are not needed
To fill a pure and muted space,
Listening is stillness.
Reflect, a new idea is near,
Grounded in thoughts of hope,
Shaped while waiting, listening, reflecting
In silence, in stillness.
Begin, a new path is near,
The circle widens with new links
Holding fast, moving forward,
No more stillness...not now.

Two years passed. The People to People Citizens Ambassador Program gave me an opportunity to move forward. I was invited to be a United States delegate to the Joint International Early Childhood Conference, at Beijing Normal University, in Beijing, China, the capital city. Drs. Richard M. Gargiulo, and Stephen B. Graves (University of Alabama at Birmingham) led the two hundred-member United States delegation of early childhood professionals during the ten-day conference.

I wrote Millard and Mom on October 26, 1993, the day of arrival after an eighteen-hour non-stop flight from San Francisco.

Dear Mom,

I'm writing from a hotel in the People's Republic of China. Tomorrow, China's early childhood government officials, along with professors from Beijing University, and their students will be in working meetings with our delegation. I'll make a presentation at the teacher preparation session and speak through a Chinese interpreter. My talk's about the Birt-Educare Curriculum I designed for the Martha C. Cummings Child Development Center in Zwide, South Africa. Mom, I especially want to emphasize that geographic, socio-political, and economic boundaries throughout the world, can be transcended in order to help children.

Love, Marguerite

Hi Honey,

Today, we went to Tian'man Square. It felt strange walking there knowing that hundreds of young Chinese students were recently killed by the army and some imprisoned by the Chinese government for demonstrating against the governments' restrictions on human rights. From the Square one can see the Great Hall of the People. We'll go there for dinner tomorrow night.

Already, a group of African-American women have bonded. While we were in the Square, almost immediately, Chinese people, mostly all of them dressed in the same shade of green, surrounded us and stared. We stared back, and got attitudes. Each time they encircled us we pushed past them. Later, we were told they wanted to look closer at our skin and features.

Marguerite

Dear Honey,

A school band of Chinese children welcomed us as we processed into the Great Hall. It's 10,117 feet from north to south and has a 328-foot marble floor. Alexander Pushkin and Lenin were once here, I thought and gazed at the stage where Stalin, Khrushchev, Brezhnev, and the more peaceful, Gorbachev, once sat. Millard, at dinner, before eating, I bowed my head and silently said grace. Chinese guests were seated at each of the tables, and those at our table paid no attention to me. But, an American woman came over. She touched my arm and said, "I prayed, too." Tomorrow we leave for the Forbidden City and the Summer Palace.

Love You

Dear Mom,

Any physical or mental impairment is regarded as imperfections that detract from China's regard for their ethnic purity and superiority. Imperfections shame the Chinese. This is probably why people with visible handicaps were rarely seen in the city, or countryside. We visited a facility for mildly handicapped children, and the most we saw from the many children there was a six-year-old boy with a missing finger. Although we saw buildings further away on the grounds, and people around them, we were not permitted to visit.

Travel is on foot, bikes, buses and in compact cars. People walk in crowds, and those who can own bikes. Already, we've decided to give our student guide enough money to buy a bike (she broke down in tears). She needed to save for two years to afford one.

In the country, farmers ride in open carts that overflow with cabbage. Remember the underwear you bought for us with the buttoned-

down flap in the back? That's what little children wear. They move off the roads, lower the flap, and relieve themselves. Peoples' feces and cow manure are collected on wagons, and used to fertilize farmlands.
Your daughter,

Dear Mom,
China is a large country. It is hard to believe that Japan once wanted to rule it. Mom how could a country as small as Japan attack America by attacking Pearl Harbor ?
I bet Daddy wanted to know that answer when he was fighting the Japanese in Germany. Do you think he even knew the difference between a Chinese and a Japanese? He was so far from home. Next stop, Fragrant City.
Your daughter,

Hi Honey,
I was standing at a souvenir booth in a clearing before continuing up another higher level of steps at the Great Wall...just looking and not touching the badly made figurines like, "G.I. Joe," when a scam started. Plaster statues were shattered beside my feet when two Chinese threw them to the ground and began screaming, "SHE BREAK! SHE PAY!, SHE BREAK! SHE PAY!" They held MY arm and pulled MY purse strap. A sister in our group rushed over, and began out screaming the pair in Chinese. She snatched my arm away from them. "Hold onto your bag, they want your money." Slowly, we walked out of the angry crowd that gathered, and back into the tour bus. "What did you say to make them stop ?" "TAKE YOUR DAMN HANDS OFF HER, OR I'LL BLOW YOUR SHITHEADS OFF. MOVE ASSHOLES, MOVE! Cussing and spitting is an international language," she said.
Marguerite

Dear Mom,
This is our last day here. Each morning I looked out my hotel window to see men and women and young children in pairs doing movements called Tai Chi. It is so graceful to watch...they seem to be dancing in slow motion. As a backdrop to this, I have heard in the far distance chantings to Buddah, and much closer to the hotel, cadence shouted by China's army units in their early morning drills. Dancing, praying, waring ...I heard someone say years ago, "the way we rear children determines largely whether we have war or peace ..." I do believe this.
Mom, I will dance and pray and teach peace, as you taught it to us.
Thanks, Marguerite

The letters to Millard and Mom were mailed to them *after* I came home to America.

CHAPTER 8

What is it about leaving your surroundings that make you appreciate them even more when you return? China, did this for me.

LOVING HIM

As I reflected upon my marriage to Millard, I began to realize how much his life as a minister had influenced my spiritual growth. For eighteen years I witnessed and participated in the rituals of the church like Holy Communion, receiving members into full membership, baptism of infants, marriage ceremonies, ordinations, and burial of the dead.

Reverend Birt had a sincere reverence for his ministry. Every first Sunday, at the Service of the Lord's Supper, he dressed in his white robe. As he knelt beside the white linen-covered table, set with the sacraments of bread and wine, he would lead the general confession. Afterwards, he raised the bread in his hand and said "...I eat it." He paused for a minute before eating the bread. Then, he raised the small cup of wine in his hand, looked at it, and said, "...I drink it." Again he paused, then drank the wine. His way of pausing before taking the sacraments gave more time for reflection. Those who did not have time for this most sacred service would already have left the sanctuary by courtesy of the ushers, leaving those of us who stayed - renewed.

When he baptized a baby, he cradled the infant in his left arm, and gently straightened its pristine white outfit. If the baby was crying, it stopped, I think, because Reverend Birt looked right into its eyes. Then, he addressed the parents and guardians of their responsibilities to the child. After their responses to "Name this child" he gathered water from the baptismal fount, and gently released it from his cupped hand over the baby's head. The water was wiped away with a white cloth. Both of his massive hands held the baby high in the air until the child faced the standing congregation who sighed in unison, "AAAAHHHHH."

Engaged couples were counseled over months before the wedding, but to my knowledge he never went to the wedding rehearsal. On the day of the ceremony, he waited for the couple at the altar. Later in the ceremony, he held their rings in his hand and compared their union to an unbroken circle.

"Marriage is for the rest of your lives, and the wedding is one day," he said to couples. He wanted their full attention at the marriage ceremony. Even when his daughter Cecelia was married at Mt. Teman, he did not attend the rehearsal.

An AME Ordination service is unforgettable. Members of the candidate's family cry out with thanksgiving during the preaching because it is a long laborious time between accepting God's call, and spiritual scholarly preparation for his service. When the time finally comes and itinerant ministers cluster at the altar and stack their hands on the candidate's head that is when one really hear shouts of joy!

The joys of weddings, baptisms, and ordinations, must sustain ministers during times of illness, death, and funerals. Each time Reverend Birt eulogized a church member, he recited from memory, "...I am the Resurrection and the Light, said the Lord: he that believeth in me though he were dead, yet shall he live; and whosoever liveth and believeth in me shall never die." It was the never die part that grounded my faith.

From the pulpit, he looked at the bereaved and said, "You're not looking at your loved one in that coffin. She's not there. Her feet have struck the shores of Zion, and she's gone home to be with the Lord."

When their sisters died, first Rosa, and years later Beulah; Millard, Garvin, Georgia Mae, and family, sat on the front pew at Bethel Tabernacle in Brooklyn and heard the minister ask "...O death where is your victory... ?" As the hymn was sung, Millard raised his hand and joined in singing *All is Well* as tears rolled down his chin. His faith in God's promises was a testimony that increased my faith. I began to imitate his way of being still while he waited and watched God's work. I, too, was recognizing God's work in my life.

Before we married someone warned me, "You know he's a womanizer." At first, I tried to see and hear everything. Once, I hid in his office closet behind some of his clergy robes thinking I might overhear a secret telephone conversation. Nothing! Then, after finding a matchbook from a hotel in one of his shirt pockets, I drove to the hotel and waited outside in Josephine. Nothing! When I saw a certain woman go into his office, I climbed a small tree by his office window, and peeped like Tom. I fell as the branch bent, and came to my senses that very moment while sitting on the ground in my white lace gloves, and prayer cap.

A light came on in my eyes as I began to REALLY read with a new understanding from my collection of marriage and family relations books that I had used for years to plan lectures for my classes at Queens. I began reading for my own personal needs. Marriage and Family Relations is a field of study. It is not like it was fifty years ago. Now, it is regarded as an academic discipline, and can be studied from the perspective of sociology, psychology, economics, mental health, foods and nutrition, education, and moral ethics. My mind opened. After reading materials in my secular books, I would turn pages in my Bible and my eyes would focus on the perfect lesson – giving insight that strengthened and empowered me. With discernment, slowly I began to focus on three facts - God sees everything, I loved Millard, and he loved me.

Expensive cars and speeding is also empowering to some people.

"Mrs. Birt," a senior lady of the church said, "Reverend Birt's got a heavy foot. He drives TOO FAST."

Another said, "I duck behind the first apartment steps I can find after prayer meeting, so he won't see me. I try my best to beat him before he gets outside. The last time he gave me a ride home to the Bronx I almost had a heart attack. I'm telling you the truth, my toes were 'bout numb from putting on brakes the whole time."

Even Mary Kitt warned him, "Reveren' I'm ridin' witch ya toda' witch ya HARD-HEADED SELF. Miss Birt don' even ride witch ya. She ain' crazy. Don' ya fool 'round and have no accident, with me in ya car."

They did not know about his wild driving in Wrens and how children jumped off the road when they saw him, and yelled - "WATCH OUT, HERECOMEMILLABIRT!" He still liked to drive fast, and more incredible, he had never had an accident.

The day he called saying, "Marguerite, I'm down here at the dealers' they're bringing me home, I had an accident," I was beside myself.

"An accident - Are you hurt ?"

"No, but the Jetta is a total wreck."

Amanda and I rushed to the front steps to wait for him. When he got out of the courtesy car Amanda ran to him.

"What happened, Dad.?"

"Were you hurt Millard ?," He slumped into a chair.

"An eighteen wheeler hit me on the driver's side. That thing hit me so hard I went from one lane to another. Other cars saw him hit me, and he kept on going. I don't think he even saw me when he changed lanes. It's a wonder I didn't hit anyone, and no one hit me. He hit me with so much force I COULDN'T stop. I held onto that wheel though…"

Amanda was sitting in his lap listening in awe.

"When I pulled over, lots of people stopped and came to help me. A lady from Co-op City gave me a ride to the body shop. They went to tow in the car."

Finally, the three of us walked into the kitchen.

"You could have been killed, Millard."

"Dad, you could have been killed," Amanda repeated, as she opened his glocous kit and dabbed at the small cut on his head with an alcohol wipe, and held his hand in hers.

I put his damp head against my breast, and kissed it.

"Well," he said, "let me get on to prayer meeting."

"Don't you feel a little light-headed, Millard. Should you be going back out there?"

"Yup."
He got the keys to the Benz and left.

The Birts, New York City

Success is also known to make one feel light-headed. Under the astute leadership of Bishop Cummings, and the monitoring of Self Help, Inc., the First District headquarters became a success story. WHAT PRIDE!! The property is a 120,000 square foot three story building in the University City area at 38th and Market Streets in Philadelphia. There is commercial space, and a convention center for conferences, receptions, banquets, and meetings.

The First District Plaza is the legacy of Bishop & Mrs. Cummings made possible by God's goodness, and the people of the district who worked at the local, area, and conference levels to make a vision a reality.

When my family and friends who are not AME ask me about the AME church, I try to tell them about my learning experiences in the church. It is a connectional body, divided into nineteen geographic locations called districts. Each district is presided over by a bishop elected by a majority of delegates at the General Conference, which convenes every four years in a designated city. Bishops serve in a district for eight years. One of the strengths of the church is every component of it is connected to form the whole. There is an organizational structure called levels comprised of local, area, conference, district, and the connectional. The bond that holds the connections between the levels are God's goodness, the church's history, its people, its purposes, and its resources. Worship in an AME Church at 10:45 on a Sunday morning anywhere in the world, and one is likely to follow the same order of service, sing the same hymns, talk about the same bishops, connectional officers, and meetings, even if they are speaking in Twi, Swahili or Geechee.

The connection is more than an organizational format. I have described it as being a mirror at the top of the dresser reflecting the work and service accomplished in the district, conference, area, and local church. This model is top-down, and driven by the bishop's goals. The work and service is more authentic when it is in reverse order beginning in the local church, continuing in the area, conference, district, and then the connection. I call this model bottom-up and it is also driven by the bishop's goals.

An AME who is the child of AME parents and grandparents has a distinct title called *AME born and bred*. For some, this legacy extends from earlier generations such as Bishop Nichols' wife, Mrs. Kay Bailey Nichols, being the great-great granddaughter of Frederick Douglas. The lineage is a valued connection, and carries with it prestige, privileges, and promises of well-placed assignments in the church's strata.

AMEs are quick to say, "…This is us's Church…" This can have many interpretations, which is why the *Discipline* of the Church is critical to its governance. It was first published in 1817. It is a descriptive and binding compilation of principles that define the practices of bishops, cleric and laity. Through the years, when scholars, theologians, historians, and linguists, examine the *Discipline*, there is astonishment over the vision of the early church leaders and the clarity of their language and collective purposes. If one looks at a *Discipline* of today, and any others from previous years, its evolution holds firmly to the intentions and principles written by the sons of slaves. The church's beliefs, commitments, and rules are connected and documented plainly in its book of law.

Millard served under several bishops during his pastorate. Since our marriage in 1976, he served under four administrations - Bishops Hickman, Hildebrand, Cummings, and Cousin. Bishop Ernest Lawrence Hickman presided over the First District. (1972-1976), and joined us in marriage. His wife, Mrs. Cleopatra Hickman, was the Episcopal Supervisor. Bishop Hickman preached powerful sermons. He had a child-like laugh and was openly attentive to Mrs. Hickman, whom he called Babe.

Bishop Richard Allen Hildebrand (1976-1984) served after Bishop Hickman. Beatrix Hildebrand, his wife, was the Episcopal Supervisor. Bishop Hildebrand brought the Youth Congress in Dover, Delaware, to new life when he appointed Reverend Floyd Flake director. The Congress changed leadership and programming to reflect a more inclusive focus upon christian education for children, youth, adults, and clergy. The Wilmington, Delaware, Learning Experience began as an outgrowth of the District Executive Board meeting held each year in January. Doris Garcia and Marion Tyson (Mrs. Albert D. Tyson, Jr.) were two of the original group members to coordinate plans for the first Learning Experience.

Ruth Hughes served as president of the Women's Missionary Society of the First Episcopal District twice since her first election to this office in 1971. Afterwhich, Virginia Martin was appointed president and served for nearly three months, when Ruth Hughes was reappointed president. Mrs. Hugh's unique, irascible, New York City-style, complemented the implementation of women's programming during Bishop Hildebrand's administration.

Bishop Frank Curtis Cummings presided over the First District (1984-1993). Bishop Cummings served previously as Secretary-Treasurer of the Department of Church Extension before his election to the bench. His proven reputation as a caring churchman, administrator, strategic financial planner, and visionary led the district to accomplish many firsts. Among them were the planning, funding and construction of the First District Plaza.

Martha Cummings, Episcopal Supervisor, was formerly a lieutenant junior grade officer in the United States Navy Nursing Corps. Bishop calls her Angel. She raised our commitment to building strong families, and extended our mission field to South Africa, where a child development center was rebuilt and named in her honor.

Bishop Phillip R. Cousin was the next prelate of the First District. As the former President of Kittrell College in North Carolina, he encouraged academic achievement in the clergy. Joan Cousin, Episcopal Supervisor has a refreshing sense of humor and a commitment to recruiting more "young legs" (young women) into the local church, and the Women's Missionary Society. She motivated the missionaries to educate congregations about HIV/AIDS.

In reflection, each Bishop initiated programs and practices that best represented his vision for the district, and the church. I tell those who ask about my church there is one aspect that is always observable, regardless of who the bishop is, there is an URGENCY to work and serve. Each one, so to speak, hits the ground running. It is dangerous to miss any meetings called by the bishop.

In time, Reverend Albert D. Tyson, Jr., was transferred from New Jersey to the New York Conference and assigned to Macedonia in Flushing, not far from Queens College. The Tysons were welcomed additions to a growing circle of trustworthy supporters. On some Sunday nights, Millard and Reverend Tyson talked about their sermons on the telephone, as they had done for years. Later, there would be seriousness as they critiqued each other's day. By now, I had come to know Margaret Tyson. I still remember her in that white galebao, walking with her Chad students on Newark's Clinton Avenue. She was a fiery and compassionate teacher.

Once, as I prepared for a trip, I asked Margaret to lecture to my class at Queens. At the time, Amy Fisher, a Long Island teenager, was being prosecuted for the near-fatal shooting of Joey Butufuco's wife. The frenzied media called Amy the Long Island Lolita. Her mother was always at her side. Amy testified that she and Butofuco had an affair. She told the court she went to the Butofuco's home with a gun to scare his wife, but the gun went off accidentally. Mrs. Butofuco was wounded in the face and head, and Amy was convicted and sentenced to prison.

The chairlady of the home economics department called me into her office, "Dr. Birt, Amy Fisher's mother is a student in this department. She's a senior and ready to graduate after she takes your class. She needs as much privacy as possible - her life is hell right now. Can you handle it ?"

I could.

When Margaret lectured, she did not know that Mrs. Fisher would be one of thirty-eight students. Mrs. Fisher would be the first to arrive, and sit on the front row closest to the door. She never spoke in class, but wrote detailed and insightful papers. To this day, I doubt that Margaret knew she was there.

I wanted a private talk with Mrs. Fisher, and one evening, before students arrived, I asked, "Mrs. Fisher, I don't mean to impose upon you, and you don't have to answer...we have a daughter in middle school, I've seen you on television with your daughter, and when I read your essays, you have strong convictions about being a mother. What is your advice?"

"Are you married, Dr. Birt?"

"Yes, my husband is a minister."

"You probably know my husband is in the upholstery business."

She looked at me from under a beige rain hat, got up, closed my office door and talked to me.

Uncle Junnie and Amanda

Our daughter was growing up. Elsie Howard, her godmother in Somerset, New Jersey, Charlotte Gipson, my brother (Uncle Junnie), and I, talked over the years about Amanda. She was thirteen now, in Catholic school, in smaller classes, and receiving more quality attention from her teachers. She went to chapel daily. She was developing a stronger sense of God in her life. She and her Dad were very close. Amanda rode with him more frequently than she rode with me, knew short cuts in Harlem, and every bridge into Manhattan. She knew where AME churches were in the Bronx, and in other boroughs.

We used to ride in one car to church when we first came to

Emanuel. She was only five then. We traveled up Park Avenue and would pass 125th Street, where prostitutes picked up customers, especially on Sundays. I remember telling her, "Those ladies are waiting for their friends," when she asked us, "What are they doing?"

I planned to tell her more, as she got older.

"Amanda, you stopped asking me years ago about those ladies on Park Avenue. Do you remember what I told you about them?"

"Yes. Dad and I used to laugh about you saying, 'They're waiting for their friends.' He told me they're prostitutes and sell their bodies, and half the time they don't know who they get in cars with. Dad told me lots of stuff when he carried me to YPD meetings and A & P. He said you tell me things in your own way, and he tells me things in his way, and that both ways are O.K."

"God hates sin, but he loves the sinner. Did you ever hear that?"

"Yes, Amanda."

"You know what else he said?"

"What?"

"You have no sense of direction."

"He's right."

"I know, that's why I help you when you're lost. I tell Dad when I hear funny sounds in your car, too."

That day, I realized the valuable lessons he had already taught our teenager. I thought of one thing Mrs. Fisher told me, "Make your daughter take her time to grow up."

One night Amanda asked, "Dad, do you think Bishop's going to move us again?"

"The Bishop can move me anytime, he needs to. Why...you ready to leave New York?"

"No, but if we move, me and Tehera promised to be friends forever. We're going to college together, and get our apartment together in New York."

That's good. What college are you going to?" he asked.

"I don't know yet. First, we need to decide where's the best place for young Black women to live in New York"

"Why do you say Black women?" I asked.

"Mom, remember that Sunday morning we were getting out the car and this addict was in front of the church putting a needle in his arm? He said 'Pray for me' when you pushed my window up, and told me, "Wait...don't get out."

"I remember."

"Well, that worries me. If I live in New York, I don't want any drug addicts around my apartment. And another thing that worries me…the night we went to see Phyllis (Dru's daughter) dance in Alvin Ailey's Company at City Center, afterwards, we couldn't get a cab to take us to Grand Central Station to get a train back to New Rochelle. Remember us catching a bus, and me with that bunch of flowers Alvin Ailey's Mom gave me when Phyllis introduced us to her and to Judith Jameison. I remember all those taxis passed right by us because we were Black. When we got to New Rochelle, it was really late."

"When did all of this happen…I never heard about the cabs?"

Millard's question gave me time to think of an answer.

Millard wanted to protect us, and he would have been satisfied if we never ventured beyond where he thought it was safe for us. I knew that kind of protection could limit our thinking, and the possibility of choosing options. This kind of protection would make us completely dependent upon him, not able to think for ourselves, and if the time ever came when he needed to rely on us, we might be too scared of everything to help him…so Amanda and I ventured - together and separately.

"I was nine then," said Amanda.

"And a sharp nine, too. Tell your father about the day we were shopping in Scarsdale. This young white girl got out of her mother's jaguar, and pretended to walk away, until she saw her mother go into Bond's."

"Yeah, I saw her go between Bond's and Lord & Taylor, and this man just went to her, and started tying this thing around her arm. He gave her a shot with a needle, and she got right back in her car. Her mother didn't even know."

"It happened in Scarsdale right?…one of the richest places in Westchester. Amanda, drug addicts are everywhere. You have to be careful of people wherever you are. You first need to decide what you want to be and what college you want to go to. She'll need money to live in New York, right Millard? That night we couldn't get a cab, we went to plan B…always have plan B, Amanda. We wanted to get back to New Rochelle. I bet the people on the bus thought you were special with those pretty flowers…we had fun didn't we?"

"Millard, if Amanda becomes a lawyer she could work to make things better for Black people, couldn't she?"

"You going to be a lawyer, Squeeko?" he bit on his pipe.

"I don't know, I think I might be a gynecologist."

Seasons passed and passed.

Then, it happened. It was January 1995, and Amanda was fifteen.

She found him slumped in a chair in the living room.

He recuperated with rest and therapy. Fastina Brown, our house-keeper and friend, was living with us full time. Althea and Cecelia came to New Rochelle, almost every weekend. The girls helped in ways that adult daughters can. When he became well enough to preach at Emanuel again, to monitor his meals, I wrote a sign and placed it in the church kitchen.

Thank you for preparing low salt foods
to serve Reverend Birt at the pastor's table.
The Birt Family

When he saw the sign he did not like it.

Millard resumed attending First District services and meetings. Reverends Robert A. Brown, Jr., Wayne A. Johnson, Sr., and James E. F. Lawrence often drove him to places in his SEL 500 Mercedes Benz…it was loaded, and had 315 horsepower under the hood. When he returned to New Rochelle, from wherever he had gone, because his blood sugar plummeted either too high or too low… one of them drove him home FAST!!

By now, I was assistant professor of early childhood education at York College in Jamaica, New York. Josephine Dunbar Davis, was president, and the first woman of color to head a City University of New York institution. Dr. Davis fostered alignment between York College, and the political, economic, and cultural missions within the African-American, Asian, Caribbean, and Latinos groups that made up the diverse community. She was actively pursuing global partnerships between York College and key universities in Ghana, West Africa, and China. To this end, she and a York College delegation had traveled to both countries, and collaborations for a reciprocal student and faculty exchange program was in progress.

York College is in the same vibrant community as Allen AME Church, where Reverend Floyd Flake, Jr., a former college president himself and now a United States Congressman continued to serve as senior pastor. Many of Allen's members are students at York College. There was supportive alignment between Dr. Davis and Congressman Flake when it came to the best interests of students.

Some York College faculty and staff members took exception to Dr. Davis. When she appointed me, a freshman faculty person, over senior department faculty to chair a blue ribbon committee on teacher education it triggered mayhem. Over the months that followed the appointment was put on hold.

Meanwhile, I submitted a proposal that was funded by the American Association of University Women to research infusing Chinese culture into the early childhood curriculum. It was impossible to overlook the blatant, sometimes subtle political, social, economic, and cultural ways in which other ethnic members, who lived or had thriving businesses in Jamaica, Queens, tended to relate to some Blacks. I organized my concerns, collected data, and designed a project that introduced prospective early childhood teachers to techniques of presenting Chinese artifacts to school children during their student teaching. I proposed that collections of Chinese artifacts could be taken into classrooms, examined by the children, and the student teachers could use these materials to teach about aspects of Chinese culture. I remembered how the Chinese children on Harmon Street in Savannah looked at me, and I looked at them from a distance. We were in the twentieth century with technology having made the world and the people in it geographically closer, yet we continue to grapple with our misperceptions about people near to us and those still far away.

My York College students were Asian, Latinos, Africans, African-Americans, Native Americans, Caucasians, and Europeans. Some had roots from the Caribbean, and other islands. In class, as we prepared to teach children in the city's schools, we were also learning valuable lessons that we could transmit to our own families, and within the communities where we lived, shopped, socialized and worshiped.

During the summer, I joined fifty-five other university researchers to study aspects of Chinese culture at the East-West Center of Asian Studies at the University of Hawaii at Mano, Honolulu. York College provided additional funding for my studies.While in Hawaii, I visited Pearl Harbor, and knew more than ever that cultural hate is an antecedent to acts of war. I would return to York College and make a difference.

I discovered that some Chinese children are reared to look aside when they speak to adults as a sign of their respect for them. Knowing this, teachers should not interpret this as being disrespectful. The Chinese practice shaming individuals as a means of controlling social and national behavior. Chinese children are often socialized to master a skill before it is publically demonstrated. Teachers can encourage children to try things, and be confident in learning how to do them. All Chinese children are not superior in their math and science abilities. This myth can cause teachers of Chinese students to overlook the individual academic limitations of students and fail in teaching to their needs. The tiny black hat known as a queue, with its long braid hanging at the back of it, offends many Chinese when it is worn. Non-Asian students were exposed to concepts of this nature. In exchange, Asian students in my classes were learning that Africans, African-Americans and West Indians want their change placed in their hands and not on the counter after they pay their money for purchases in Asian owned businesses. People of color tend to detest having a white person waited on first when they are rightfully the next person to be served. Saying "you people" is a poor choice of words. No one of any ethnic group likes to be mistreated as an individual, because of dislikes toward the entire ethnic group.

In the midst of these encounters, charges of financial misman-agement and misuse of administrative powers were leveled at President Davis. The charges against her and the efforts to unseat Dr. Davis polar-ized York College and Jamaica's community factions. When I failed to receive tenure, I was secretly informed it was due to the top-down appointment of me to the education committee and the belief that my husband was one of the ministers who rallied on campus, and aggres-sively supported President Davis. Millard was still mending at home, so the allegation of him participating in the campus demonstrations annoyed me. I learned later, that even my phone calls were monitored. I was in deep trouble for my association with President Davis, and my hus-band.

The New York Annual Conference met in May 1994 at Allen Jamaica. The Sunday closing service was held at York College where I sat in the auditorium with hundreds of AMEs. As I looked across the room, I could see my husband's head above other ministers. President Davis welcomed Bishop & Mrs. Cousin and the members of the Conference to York College. As I remember, she said, "Bishop Cousin I am facing strong opposition against the work we are doing at York College. We want to prepare our students to get jobs when they graduate from here. We want them to be successful and happy with their lives. I need your prayers to continue this work."

Early the next morning, James Wynne, York College professor, was struck and killed by a taxi driver as he crossed Guy R. Brewer Boulevard in front of the campus. Dr. Wynne was a brilliant math pro-fessor, and well respected by some students and faculty. He was a union man, and did not support President Davis. On several occasions, he was invited to our department meetings as an interested party. I recall at one meeting, he asked me, "How did President Davis appoint you to chair the education committee ?"

No one asked me a single question over the months of department meetings. I waited and anticipated this question.

The eight department members were sitting around the conference table waiting for my reply.

"I cannot tell you HOW Dr. Davis appointed me, but I can tell you WHY. She read my vitae, as surely as she read each of yours, and felt confident of my leadership." Their white faces turned red.

As I sat in my office the morning of Dr. Wynne's tragic death, I thought of his question to me. He asked what he had to. I did not blame him because it gave me an opportunity to answer. Moreover, I was AME, I would forgive, but I needed time to forget… and it was still, too soon.

CHAPTER 9

President Josephine Davis resigned from York College, and received a professorial position at Queens College. I left York College and continued as adjunct at Queens. Sadly, Millard's diabetes worsened.

KNOWING WHEN TO LEAVE THE PARTY

"Did you see me this morning?" he asked.

Yes, I had seen him, and knew he did not trust himself to lift the baby he had just baptized into the air the way he usually did. He did not have the strength in his hands to do it. I could not begin to count the times he had safely lifted infants into the air. He also lifted me up. Perhaps, the truthful and loving way a minister introduces his wife to an audience is a way of lifting her up mentally and emotionally. No one else can do it like a woman's husband.

Most wives of ministers have a designated place to sit in their congregation. There are pros and cons about this issue. Some say no one owns a seat in the church unless they have paid for that seat on the pew. They should not expect to sit in the same seat every Sunday. Others say, if the minister's wife sits in the same seat, visitors will know who she is, and where she can be found. From experience, when I sat in places other than down front I heard all kinds of remarks. It happened to me at conference and district level sessions when I was newly wed, and no one knew I was Mrs.Birt. I heard too much, and thought it best to sit down front with my sisters just in case they started to discuss my husband.

An AME usher had us laughing at a district service, when she said, "Y'all minister's wives better get in your seats and stay in them, before some of these preacher's girlfriends get in them. They are very nervy, and don't mind asking the ushers to "…please seat me." I ask them, "WHO YOU?" Y'all know, if we tried to seat all of the girlfriends, y'all sure wouldn't have no place to sit for real."

Somewhere we heard the statement, "No one can take your place, as long as you are IN IT."

But, we also heard, "Some women, don't want to marry your husband, and be a preacher's wife, they just want to BE with him, and the sneakier it is the more fun it is."

When ministers' wives worship together or attend an event as a group, there is usually designated seating, and often special recognition, such as "...Will all of the ministers' wives stand." To me, this has always been an appreciated acknowledgement. I was proud to be an AME minister's wife. It can be an effective tool for a ministers' wife to flaunt, "I am his wife," when wannabes try to unseat her.

Ministers' wives like to sit shoulder to shoulder, and kiss each other on the cheek as they greet, bending down under each other's hats when they want to say something. Often, wives of ministers stand slowly when they are presented, skim the back of their outfits with their hands, and turn their heads to the left and right, facing the audience, and smiling broadly.

The thoughtful thing to be said of us is "...Will all ministers wives and widows please stand..." When we stand, we can be warriors as most are committed wives, mothers and churchwomen. One can confide in us. Every closed eye is not asleep, we see and do not see, and do not mistake quietness for anything than what it is. We ask others do not underestimate our perfect timing of assertiveness, and do not mistreat our children. The children cannot handle the harsh treatment like their fathers can. The Lord knows that most ministers' wives know what to pray for.

Whenever a minister's wife dresses for a worship service, people expect her to be in a preacher's wife's outfit with a hat on. Do not ask me what those combinations look like, except, the outfit should not be too short, too tight, or too flimsy. More flesh should be in, than out, so when the male ushers take up collection at a wife's end row seat they do not linger at her row too long. If she has wide hips, and does not like to control her side or back movements, all heads, female and male, will turn in her direction when she goes to and from the altar. Women can be heard thinking – "Why doesn't she just sit herself down..." In some ways, a minister's wife's clothes, her walk, and her mouth can do much good or very much damage.

"Oh, Millard," I said one Christmas, "thank you for this SHARP SUIT AND HAT." He gave me an off white felt hat and a four piece off white woolen suit with a slim skirt, stopping just at my knees. There was a matching black and white silk blouse. The hat was a *Mr. John* with long, beautiful black feathers that started at the front of the hat. If I rolled my eyes to the right side as far as they would go, I could see the feathers bobbing up and down. It was shaped like a cowboy's hat, and whenever I wore it, he tilted it over my right eye and said, "There."

I had a clear idea of what a minister's wife should wear from the nice clothes and jewelry he bought for me. Incidentally, that was the same Christmas he gave me an electric mixer with all of the attachments.

I wore that suit and hat, as often as I used the electric mixer, which was not often. However, when I did both – wear the suit and mix a cake – I was pleased with myself, and so was he.

Lee Crumpley was a gourmet cook. She always dressed elegantly. When we became close friends, she gave me her testimonies about life and suitcases of outfits, including her hats. Lee was loved by Emanuel because she sincerely cared about others, and knew how to talk to people. When the Crumpleys came to worship at Emanuel, they needed three rows for the family to be seated. Their faces, the children and the adults showed their love for her. One thing I did not like to see was Lee Crumpley wipe tears from her eyes. It hurt to see her cry. I cry often during worship…sometimes I cry for joy, and sometimes because I am hurting. We preferred to see Lee smiling. She was so strong in her faith. Whenever she did cry she must have been really hurting.

I told Lee about something that I overheard and did not like.

Once, I called a minister's home to speak with his wife about a meeting. He put the receiver down to tell her she had a call. When she picked up, he forgot to go back to his phone and hang up. I nearly died when I heard him yelling at his wife - "Why in hell's name do you always take so damn long to pick up the damn phone. I get sick and tired of stopping what I'm doing to find you, to answer the phone. Get your own damn phone anyway. Come on in here, and answer this thing. I am not your damn secretary…" When she spoke to me it was as though nothing had been said to her. I told Lee since that incident, whenever I saw that minister and he presented his wife to an audience, I listened as he lifted her up with glowing praise and loving words, and I hoped he choked.

There is an expected protocol to follow when presenting the presiding bishop of the district, who is the main preacher at a worship service, or a bishop visiting the district, who will preach at the service. If there are several bishops present, one has to acknowledge the hierarchy of time on the bench. When there are connectional officers present in an AME worship service, or the preacher who is the speaker at an AME program when the presiding prelate of the host district is present, as well as other bishops and connectional officers, the person who is to preach is expected to call the names in the hierarchical order of their tenure and duty.

The protocol that is established transcends them being recognized in the pulpit, or on a dais. Their recognition duly defines the Body of the Connectional church that is present at that time. Who is present is as important to the occasion as who is not present. Historically, the amount of time used to identify the Body present reveals much about the person who is making the acknowledgements sometimes more than the individual who is actually delivering the message or sermon. If a person wants to see the feathers hit the fan, let someone bungle this AME greeting tradition and it is then discussed by others in a negative manner for a long time – to some; it is that serious.

When Amanda was asked to introduce Oneida Stevenson as the Manhattan District YPD candidate in the 1995 Youth of the Year contest in New York, I was nervous. She had heard her father present bishops before; connectional officers, district officers, and other clergy as well. She watched me as second vice president of the Women's Missionary Society. Amanda had countless opportunities to watch and learn, but we could not take any chances because we wanted Oneida to win.

Gloria Mackey met with Amanda and Oneida, and coached them on Amanda's introduction, and Oneida's speech, up to an hour before they went to the pulpit. I sat in the audience that night and heard our daughter reverently and correctly observe the protocol, as no other presenter before her had done. When Amanda turned her body, and held out her hand to Oneida, who stepped up to the podium, and began her speech - the energy between them connected with the audience. We were on our feet applauding them on. That is another special kind of connection experienced when AMEs, young and old, work together as a team toward a shared goal. I had goose bumps. We knew Manhattan North had won before the announcement was made. Gloria and I smiled at each other from across the sanctuary.

As I waited in the audience for Amanda, I overheard several people answer, when they were asked, "THAT WAS REVEREND BIRT'S DAUGHTHER." That night, Amanda rushed home to tell her father about what she did, and that Oneida won the contest. He had to leave the church early because he did not feel well.

"They already called and told me about you, Amanda. I like that," he said.

Later on, I witnessed something that will stay with me for the rest of my life. I saw him stand at the lectern to make his pastor's report at the 145th Session of the New York Annual Conference at Bethel, the Mackey's church. Bishop Cousin was seated inside of the chancel. Millard faced the Bishop at his left and spoke to him, "Bishop Cousin, I have served my Church to the very best of my ability. I am grateful to God that I have had fifty-five years of what I would call a fruitful ministry, but I am not well. You know that Sir. So, send me wherever you need me to go Bishop, but if it is in your Godly judgment don't send me back to Emanuel. Emanuel is a great church, but they need a minister who is well to pastor them. Bishop, I will continue to serve wherever you send me."

His words came out slowly and I clung to each one of them.

Reverend Freeman went to the lectern, and said, "Sister Marguerite Birt, come down here and stand with your husband." I looked in the balcony and beckoned to Althea and Cecelia to come and stand with us. As I stood with him, I was filled with pride. I looked out into a sea of faces... some were wiping tears, others bowed their heads, and some just looked at Millard in disbelief, I imagine. What he asked of Bishop Cousin publicly was a rare request indeed. Millard's request caught many people off guard and in a way altered the Bishop's agenda, but more than anything, it relieved Bishop Cousin from HAVING TO REMOVE HIM.

I did not know Millard was going to say what he did. We had many talks late into the night about both of us retiring, about buying a house in South Jersey near the Jones' who moved to Willingsboro, or further south, near the Francis' in Pleasantville. We even looked at retirement communities. He must have spent hours thinking about what he was going to do. Knowing him, he looked at every possible angle. While he was sitting quiet and still, he was seeking God's guidance. Now he knew it was time to leave the party. For the next three days of the conference there was much speculation about who would go to Emanuel. We certainly did not know.

It was Friday, and we were sitting in the sanctuary a distance apart. Millard saw him the same moment that I did. The young minister came from the direction of Reverend Mackey's office, and sat on the pew with the other ministers. Millard turned his head from side to side until his eyes found mine. Emanuel's pastor would be Reverend David Cousin, son of Bishop & Mrs. Cousin.

That Sunday, Bishop transferred Millard to the New England Conference, to Bethel AME in Greenwich, Connecticut, the childhood church of Luther's wife, Cathy Brown Birt. Reverend David Cousin was transferred from the New Jersey Conference to Emanuel.

I stood watching my husband find Reverend Cousin in a crowd of well wishers. Then Millard and Reverend Cousin bear-hugged one another beginning a brotherly transition between the old and the new.

Within days, the Cousins came to see the parsonage. I insisted upon showing them around to the displeasure of the church officers who accompanied them. Determined, I showed them every hole, every crusted ceiling that had been there since we moved into the house. Then, Valerie Cousin and I went to the pool.

"See this pipe, it leaks gas. Don't even consider moving in until this is fixed."

We were leaving the party!

Mary Kitt, Marilee Leacock, Fastina Brown, and I, worked to leave 40 Holly Drive spotless. There were two automatic garage openers and when we finished cleaning, I left one in the parsonage and kept the other so that I could get back in to bring out several smaller boxes.

The day I returned, perhaps five days later, I could not believe my eyes. The carpet in the living room was pulled up from the floor, and turned so that the padding was seen. The corner curio was piled on top of the upturned carpet. Sections of brown wood paneling that had been above the fireplace was stripped from the walls, and that, too, was in the middle of the floor. The sofa and the two winged back chairs were thrown into another heap. I went upstairs and saw the crowbars and ladders... "MY GOODNESS, THE CONTRACTORS HAVE STARTED WORKING ALREADY!"

After we had done all of that cleaning the house was a wreck. I pressed the button on the automatic opener, placed it on the shelf inside of the garage, and ducked under the door before it closed.

As I drove to Greenwich, I was talking to myself, "They are fixing the parsonage!" I felt happy for the couple and their two young sons. But, my darker side reasoned, "They'd better fix it, that's the Bishop's son."

Weeks passed before we heard through the grapevine people were saying, "...Reverend and Mrs. Birt should be ashamed for leaving the parsonage in the mess they did." When I heard this, my pride was hurt. That is not the kind of reputation a minister's wife wants out there. Wrecking an AME parsonage is neither forgiven nor forgotten.

I called Mrs. Kitt, "We left that house clean. I hope you and Mrs. Leacock let them know how we left it. The contractors came in after us, and made the mess."

"Mrs. Birt, don' pay no 'tention to Negroes' foolishness. You don' have nothing else to worry 'bout, up there in Greenwich??"

CHAPTER 10

Blessed are the peacemakers…

"BETHEL IS THE SWEETEST PART OF MY MINISTRY…"

On our first Sunday in church, Millard spoke to a small congregation:
"I am proud to be here in this one hundred twelve year old church. Some of you might remember me conducting revival when Reverend Alvan Johnson and Sister Betty were here. I'm sure you know that Stanley and Odester Brown and the Birts are in-laws. When we came here to see Cathy and Luther get married, little did I know that one day, I'd be standing here as your pastor. I've had some sickness…I've come a long way and expect to get better. We're going to work together. Who in here believes in working together?"
The people waved their hands.
"Amen, thank you, thank you! I want you to meet my family. This is my wife, Sister Marguerite Birt, and our daughters, Althea, Cecelia and Amanda. You'll be seeing them working around here a lot, too."
After service we went to the social hall and enjoyed baked chicken casserole, seasoned with herbs, garden grown fruits and vegetables, homemade bread and punch. There were five chairs for us at the pastor's table and no one came to us the entire time we were eating.
I remembered what Mrs. Kitt said to me, and thought to myself…maybe I don't have anything to worry about.

We arrived in town in June on the heels of the explosive Greenwich High School yearbook incident in which five white seniors alledgedly wrote a racial hate message about Blacks in their '95 yearbook. Bethel Church was the site of a community meeting of Blacks and whites sponsored by the local NAACP. A grass roots coalition formed at that meeting and separated from the moderate stand taken by the NAACP. Millard spoke at the meeting and afterwards was interviewed by a Greenwich Times reporter. Millard had stopped smoking his pipes years ago and no longer had a stem to bite on. Even so his jaw muscles still tightened when someone or something angered him. The next day his comments were in the paper: "I spoke once or twice of what I thought in the meeting. Some people in town didn't think too much of the incident – they thought it wa a prank. Others were upset, like I am. We will be living here. Ou daughter will go to the high school. I believe the police and the town di "soft pedal" the incident. I didn't see that there was too much that we a Blacks could have expected. But an apology, a published apology woul have been good enough. Blacks need to regain the sense of togethernes we had when racism was even more blatant than it is now."

Alexander Perry, the treasurer of Bethel was also interviewed. Thi is what he said,

"It's powerful what he says and the way he brings his message across i everyday words. I'd like a fellowship with all the people and all th churches in town. Reverend Birt's going to bring that back."

The church had already moved us into a furnished rental house i Stamford while the parsonage was being fixed for us. Millard drove th twenty-minute trip to Greenwich to his office each day.

Bethel Church and Parsonage, Greenwich, Connecticut

Reverend Winton Hill, III and his family lived in Stamford since he wa transferred from Mt. Teman to Bethel. Very soon, Millard and Reveren Hill were inseparable. Reverend Hill usually did most of the drivin When a person saw one in a car, he saw the other. Winton, an AME mir ister, the one who followed Millard at Mt. Teman, a military chaplai with experience in comforting those in Desert Storm, he became our rar in the bush.

"Reverend Hill, tell Marguerite about Mt. Teman's parking lot after we left Elizabeth."

"Mrs. Birt, a week after Reverend Birt left Elizabeth, I got a call to finish the parking lot...city hall couldn't wait for Reverend Birt to leave town..."

The two of them laughed like they were crazy.

Within three months, Artis Roberts, Bethel's trustee, church custodian, van driver, Sunday School teacher, and professional mover moved us the third time. Finally, we moved into the ninety-nine year old parsonage beside the church.

The four-storied house was beautifully renovated, except for the church office on the first level. A gliding chair, from the second to the third floor, bypassed twenty steps. Even so, the number of other steps still concerned us. There were eighteen steps from the driveway to the parsonage backdoor, and another twelve steps on the street level leading to the front door. There were twenty-five narrow steps from the second floor into the first floor office. The steepest steps were the fifteen up to the spacious fourth floor loft, making ninety steps in all!

The kitchen was remodeled with a new stove, refrigerator, dishwasher, and washer-dryer they asked me to help select. This alone showed their respect for Millard and me. Alexander Perry, Artis Roberts, and others, installed cherry-finished kitchen wall cabinets and tediously hung new blinds throughout the house. Even the den was refurnished with a handsome sofa, a matching love seat, and reclining chair. Our own big screen television fit in perfectly. Sarah Perry, Isabelle Prester and Blanche Allen, patiently hung color-coordinated sets of curtains to each window. Some days, when I returned from work at Queens College, members were in the house working. Someone had even unpacked our books, and arranged them on the shelves in the den.

Perhaps, the sight to behold was the king-sized walk in shower in the black and white checkerboard tile bathroom! We looked in amazement.

"Millard have you ever seen people work together like this before?"

"They're something... they come together and work. All of this work, the members and their contacts did it, PEACEFULLY."

"Dad, this is so NICE," Amanda smiled.

"Yes it is, let's sit on the front porch."

The front porch was on the second floor with a clear view of the emergency entrance to the Greenwich Hospital. Whenever our members who worked in the hospital saw us on the porch they spoke:

"Hello, Reverend!"

"Hello, Mrs. Birt!"

"Hello, Amanda

The three of us waved and yelled back.

Amanda made several new friends at Greenwich High Schoo and they sat on the porch with her . Cathy, our daughter-in-law, lived wit Luther and their children in North Carolina. She graduated fron Greenwich High and knew some of the teachers who were still at th school. Cathy had lots of advice for Amanda. "Why don't you be a chee leader, like I was ?"

Odester and I had been close in-laws over the years of our chi dren's marriage. When we moved to Greenwich, it was a blessing the now we were able to spend more time talking and working together o "family matters." Odester worked as a secretary in the Greenwic Hospital and above all was a faithful member and officer at Bethel.

At noon on September 16, 1995, over twenty-five ministers of th Manhattan District led by presiding elder William Lee Freeman spo sored a service of appreciation for us at Bethel. Reverend S. Fran Emmanuel presided over the program. Presiding Elder Herbert Edd welcomed us to the New England Conference over which he preside Reverend Freeman stated the occasion: "We have come today to be wit Reverend Millard D. Birt, our friend and your pastor, Sister Margueri Birt, and Amanda. We have come to show our support from th Manhattan District…"

Millard expressed his appreciation to Reverend Freeman becaus while we were in New Rochelle, and despite his own declining health, h had faithfully visited and communed Millard. There were many others the service including Presiding Elder Ernestine Ward, the first female t be appointed a presiding elder in the First Episcopal District. Each one them supported Millard's ministry. Reverend O'Neil Mackey, S preached and afterwards the district presented Millard a monetary gif Then, Bethel served our well wishers a nutritious New England style di ner.

Three months later, on December 2, Bethel's Steward Board ga\ us a welcome reception, and Josiah Smith was the chairman. In the sho time Millard had been in Greenwich, he had reached out to leaders of th city and fellowshipped with the clergy. Tom Ragland, the first selectma of Greenwich (mayor) greeted us as did ministers from the Greenwic Port Chester, Mamaroneck Black Ministerial Alliance. The hospital female chaplain, Reverend Garlick came. Presiding Elder Eddy, an

Reverend Winton Hill were present.

Our first Christmas in Greenwich was simply beautiful. Snow covered the town and made Lake Avenue so quiet. When we came to Bethel, we were told the doors to the church were never locked. Every now and then strangers entered the church (to pray?) and left minutes later.

Amanda said, "No one in Greenwich needs to steal anything from us. People here have everything they need…"

A local florist donated two evergreen wreaths with flowing red ribbons that were placed on the front doors of the church. A Christmas tree decorated by the Christian Education Department filled the church foyer, and under the tree were gifts for children and adults. Poinsettias lined the pulpit. The mahogany woodwork throughout the sanctuary gleamed. As usual, the church had been cleaned by all of us pitching in with dust cloths, brooms, Ajax and Windex. A wreath and poinsettias were left on our porch, as well as baskets filled with homemade breads and cookies, bags of nuts, and boxes of fruits. Each morning gifts were on our porch, and we never knew who brought them to us.

Millard and the officers visited the sick and communed them. Christmas envelopes and food baskets were delivered to Bethel's homebound. All during the month, we sang Christmas carols- "Joy to the World," "O Little Town of Bethlehem," "Silent Night."

Finally, at the children's Christmas program, their choir sang "Away in a Manger."

I cannot explain that Christmas in Greenwich - I had such peace within.

In 1996, when Founder's Day came, we remembered Richard Allen's birth on February 14, 1760, when later, his parents and four of his siblings were sold into slavery in Dover, Delaware, by Benjamin Chew, their Philadelphia slave owner. All AME congregations know about our church's founding, and how in April 1816 Allen and others walked out of Philadelphia's St. George's Church. Each year we retell this story, and recommit ourselves. After the morning service, Reverend Birt, Amanda, and I, hosted the church at the parsonage. It was our way of saying thanks to them.

Two of Bethel's golden aged matriarchs; Edna Smith, the first licensed African-American cosmetologist in Greenwich, and Geneva Steadwell, a pioneer interior decorator of some of Connecticut's palatial homes, brought their many photo albums, scrapbooks, and other church memorabilia. They spread everything on tables and chairs, and Bethel's church family went down memory lane.

For Women's Day we raised over $8,000 and for Men's Day slightly less. Both services had great preachers! We went to the social hall for dinner and fellowship, and afterwards went home. After the Women and Men's Day services, Millard and I waited for the phone to ring with complaints from the members about something…ANYTHING. To our surprise, there was not one single call.

We began to look forward to our first New England Annual Conference. Reverend Richard Stenhouse of Bethel in Norwalk was host minister of the 145th Session of the New England Conference. Esther Twine was Bethel's delegate. Millard made his pastoral report to Bishop Phillip R. Cousin. On April 23rd Bishop Cousin introduced Millard to preach at the 7:00 service of the Department of Evangelism. Millard had campaigned (unsuccessfully) at the 1992 General Conference to become the Connectional director of the Department of Evangelism to follow Reverend G.H.J. Thibodeaux. Although Reverend Y. Benjamin Bruce won the election, the First District knew of Millard's aspirations.

His sermon that night ,"The Game of Life," was compared to a baseball game. Philippians 4:13, I can do all things through Christ who strengthens me…was his scripture.

He said, " …When it's your turn at bat you have to keep your eyes on the ball, and on the pitcher, and even be aware of who's already on the bases. You have to hit the ball with everything you've got and be ready to run. You have to touch each base and make it to home plate, SAFE. Sometimes, you have to slide in…but you just slide on in…no matter what it takes, you want to touch home plate…"

From the rear of the church, Reverend D. Albert Turk, the First District president of the Department of Evangelism, and others in the congregation, including Amanda and me, were on our feet shouting,

"PREACH, REVEREND BIRT, PREACH!!!"

Months later, he was admitted to the Greenwich Hospital for his heart. A tall white physician with snow-white hair attended Millard in the absence of his heart specialist, who lived next door to the parsonage. The doctor placed his thin hand on Millard's chest and bowed his head, as his lips moved in silence. The doctor was praying. Millard and I looked in wonderment, then we closed our eyes in prayer.

"THANK YOU, JESUS, THANK YOU, OH MERCIFUL FATHER," Millard declared.

The room was filled with the peace of the Holy Spirit.

One afternoon after he came home from the hospital, we were

sitting on the porch looking at the rain.

"Amanda, you've gotten the hang of things around here...how's school going?"

"Fine, I just can't wait to drive you around Greenwich. Dad, you gonna' let me drive the Scorpio or the Mercedes?"

"First, you've got to take the lessons and pass the test. Which one do you want to drive?"

"Everybody has a Mercedes, I want to drive the Scorpio."

"DEAL! You've made a good start here...without complaining about anything, not even moving three times...I like that, kid."

"But, Dad I want to stay in Greenwich to graduate. I hope we don't move until after I graduate."

"Amanda, moving's not so bad when you make up your mind about it. You can go anywhere you want to in the world, meet new people, accomplish new things and God will be there with you. Just don't move from him. Stay connected to God, that's what will matter...STAY CONNECTED TO GOD. Your Mother can tell you."

"Dad's right, Amanda."

A month later, Millard was admitted to the hospital. We visited him and prayed. Reverend Hill was there every day, in the morning and in the evening.

Reverend Eddy would drive 106 miles from Springfield, Massachusetts, and conducted the Sunday services. His wife, Evangelist Amelia Eddy, came with him. Reverend Arthur Jones came to preach from St. Marks, in Orange, New Jersey. Erma came with him. Reverend Joseph C. Robinson, from Allen, in Jamaica, New York preached at Bethel and his wife, Natosha Robinson, my Delta sister, accompanied him many Sundays.

As time passed, Amanda took the driving lessons, passed the test, and at sixteen, she kept her promise and drove into the backcountry where Greenwich's wealthiest live in mansions, and gated estates. The hills and winding roads, nestled among acres of green foliage and her Dad riding as a passenger, did not distract her. SHE WAS UNAFRAID TO VENTURE!

After each of their excursions into the backcountry, he'd tell her, "I liked that..."

The high school PTA operated a student employment center. I volunteered there and gave students information about after-school jobs at businesses that registered to hire Greenwich students. So far, Amanda had had a morning newspaper route, a job at a local radio station as a receptionist, a worker in a customized fabric store, then a shoe store clerk. Her pay and experience increased with each job change and now she was at her fifth job. Amanda used some of her earnings to pay for school needs, gas in the car, and for the calls she made to friends in New York on the parsonage phone.

"Mom, I got the job on Greenwich Avenue!"

The Avenue, as locals call it, is the main shopping street. Each store on the narrow one-way avenue is ultra expensive catering to the whims and tastes of the town's residents who live in the third richest town in the United States.

Greenwich policemen dress in white gloves and stand at each intersecting block, directing cars and pedestrians. Everyone waits on the curb until he yells, "CROSSSS!!" If you cross before he tells you, the officer shouts even louder, "WAITTT!!" Out-of-towners unfamiliar with the ritual are easily spotted.

"When are you coming to shop, Mom?

"Soon."

I was making two stops on the avenue that Friday, one to meet with our lawyer, Louise P. Pittocco, a skilled and compassionate attorney, and the other to the small store, where Amanda worked just doors away from his office. Amanda was standing beside the cashier. Someone had already trained her to wrap purchases in boxes covered with luxurious paper and to tie satin or grosgrain ribbons into the store's signature bows.

The store was filled with lacey, colorful items; satin and leather accessories, along with, linen and damasks placemats, and pillows of every size with fine cotton and embroidered shams. It looked like something out of a *House Beautiful* magazine.

"May I help you? Are you looking for something in particular?" the saleslady asked.

"Not really, I'm just looking."

I picked up a pair of beige satin, bedroom slippers, with tiny rosebuds on top of ecru lace bows at the front of each one. They looked like ballet shoes. They were $55 I should have put them down because as soon as she saw me pick them up she came back and said, "Aren't they just precious? Look, they come with a matching satin bag to pack them in when you travel. You can even carry this as an evening purse." It was $30.

I could not believe I was at the cashier with the slippers, matching bag and a hundred dollar bill in my hand. Amanda stared at me as she introduced me to the storeowner who was also the lady shadowing me, "This is my mother, Dr. Birt."

"It's so nice to meet you. Amanda, wrap this extra pretty for your Mom. Please come again."

My bill was $85. I walked out feeling absolutely awful.

Weeks later, Millard, Amanda, and I were at the dining room table.

"Yesterday a white man stole over $4,000 of merchandise from the store. He was dressed in a gray suit with a yellow polka-dot bow tie. We were all in the store when he did it. He must have put the stuff in his attaché case. They couldn't believe he took that much and nobody even noticed."

"With those prices, he didn't have to take much. Just shows you who they don't watch. Amanda, don't think they're not watching you... so be careful."

Lately, Millard's heart specialist, and the internist were making frequent house visits and watching him more closely. Millard started meeting with the officers in the parsonage. Attorney Pittocco also came to the parsonage and discussed personal business with Millard. One morning, I looked at his feet and ankles and they were swollen, more than usual. I knew I would not feel right wearing satin slippers on my feet. Besides, we had stopped attending evening affairs, and I honestly could not afford them. Without unwrapping the box, I returned them and got my money back.

Not long afterwards, Althea visited us when she returned from a vacation in Orlando, Florida. Excitedly, she raved about the houses she wanted us to see. I called our realtor friend Elsie Howard who had already shown us several houses in New Jersey. In four days, I was in Orlando with Mr. & Mrs. Luther Miller. Over the next three days a realtor with whom Elsie had arranged my appointment showed me several listings. I selected four houses and returned home to Millard with photographs of the properties, fact sheets, and pages of forms to sign.

I called Savannah.

"Mom, we are thinking about moving to Orlando."

"Marguerite, who do you know in Orlando?"

"Millard, knows quite a few people in Orlando."

"Child, you'd better move some place where you know people who can help you all. Your sister's here working in Dr. Ball's office, and Lisa's (Emma's daughter-in-law) a nurse in the hospital. There's Dotty and her family, Frank and Michael and their families. Did Millard forget all the ministers he knows here?"

Mom was right.

We even overlooked Augusta. Joseph Hobbs, Jr., MD, Millard's first cousin, is a well respected physician in Augusta. Over the years, and especially more recently, we had many telephone conversations asking for Dr. Hobbs' medical opinions. How did we forget Savannah and Augusta ? The light went on in both our heads. Elsie was called again and in days, she arranged for me to meet a realtor in Savannah. I flew home and found our house. With the New England Conference coming up, Millard began planning to request being a "located minister."

Some nights, he began to sing from the bedroom "TELL ME JESUS, IS MY NAME WRITTEN THERE ON THE PAGES SO FAIR...?" He sang all of the verses, and he sang them over and over, his strong tenor voice filling the house. Late in the night, he would sing Amanda, would join in singing from her bedroom, and together she and I would answer..."YES, YOUR NAME IS WRITTEN THERE ON THE PAGES SO FAIR..."

Soon, he was hospitalized again.

Reverend Eddy preached.

Reverend Stanley Charity of Emanuel NYC preached.

Reverend Hill visited Millard every morning and every evening

He began to come to the parsonage to talk to Amanda, and he talked to me. He became a confidant of my husband, and ministered to him when we were at home asleep.

Reverend Hill was always there with Millard.

Althea, Cecelia, Lewis, Luther, and Cathy and the children came to visit him too.

Amanda filled his room with balloons, and when he came home he brought them with him.

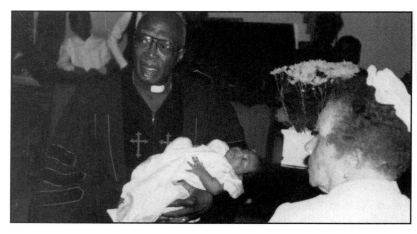

Reverend Birt baptizing Monét Foster, Sisle Crossland, the Grandmother, Bethel Greenwich (1996)

When he returned to the pulpit, he said, "Bethel is the sweetest part of my ministry. You have all done your best for my family and me. You have met every assessment, and you've faithfully carried out your duties as church officers and members. I can't say enough to thank you. Not one thing has gone undone, to my knowledge, and you work with such peaceful spirits." Then, he came down to the altar and baptized an infant girl.

For our second Christmas, the wreaths were again given to Bethel. Our porch was filled with poinsettias and homemade things. The church bought a beautiful cream-colored sofa with a matching winged-back chair. Our home smelled of pine and bayberry. Once again, Amanda had filled the live tree with all of our decorations that she knew how to hang from years of watching me.

On Christmas morning, the three of us gathered around the tree. Amanda, put on Mahaila Jackson's *Silent Night,* which was another one of our traditions.

Millard, sat in the new white high-backed chair in a burgandy velour robe.

"Let's pray," he said.

Afterwards, we each opened our gifts.

As usual, calls continued to come throughout the day, and he answered happily, "MERRY, MERRY CHRISTMAS!!"

Althea, Cecelia, and Lewis called. When he spoke to Luther, Cathy, and the grandchildren, Nathaniel, Leigha, and Katrina, he beamed with joy, as they named all they received for Christmas. Then, I heard him say to Cathy and Luther, "Bethel is the sweetest part of my ministry."

The best of all the gifts was that Cecelia offered to bring her Philadelphia theatre company to perform in Greenwich as a fundraiser for Bethel. By the day of the show we knew we would have a full audience in the 175-seat auditorium of the Greenwich Library. Cecelia portrayed Coretta King, in an original play called, "Coretta Speaks…"

It was January 23, 1997, and her father was unable to see her gifted performance… or see Althea working as her sister's business manager, or Amanda helping in the dressing room. Cecelia donated all of the proceeds to Bethel Church.

Days later, I saw his little black Bible on the bed turned to Psalm 119. I sat on the bed with him and we took turns reading the verses. Then he started to sing softly, "There is a balm in Gilead, to heal the sin-sick soul…" we harmonized together.

Shortly after the concert, Millard had surprise visitors.

"Millard, you've got some company."

I went upstairs to see if he wanted them to come up, or whether he was coming downstairs.

"Who is it?" he wanted to know.

"It's Reverend Banks (Alfred), Reverend Rhodes (Herman), and Reverend Sims (George)!!!"

"Let them come upstairs..."

They walked up the twenty steps.

"Man, I'm so glad you came," Millard beamed.

From the sofa downstairs in the den, I could hear bursts of laughter from upstairs.

His friends were ministering to him with laughter, and it filled our hearts.

Weeks later, he entered the hospital and went into a coma after three days.

On February 13, 1997, some of the people who loved Millard the most, and those whom he loved in return, met beside his hospital bed. Then, it was just Reverend Hill, Odester, Amanda and me.

Then, it was just me.

Early the next morning on February 14, 1997 at 9:15, God's servant, Reverend Millard D. Birt, closed his eyes and died. My husband's feet struck the shores of Zion, and he went home to be with the Lord.

Epilogue

So in one sense, the effective ministry has come to an end; but in another sense, the life he lived with great courage and adventure and faithfulness to his calling, is the legacy that lives on.

"M.D.", as he was affectionately known amongst his colleagues and friends, set a high standard in terms of the ministry of The Word declared with courage and conviction.

Early in his ministry in the state of Georgia after several years of successful pastorates, disaster struck. He encountered an extremely difficult situation that forced him to leave the state of Georgia and migrate to New York City. These were lean days for M.D. (career wise); it was almost like starting over for him. He never complained; he found other secular employment to support his family.

This story, as told in this book by his wife, Marguerite Birt, illustrates his God-given, uncanny ability to persevere against the odds. This is the saga of a man that loved God and loved life. This is the journey of a man, a real man with real "old-fashioned values". He always took great pride in his children and made every effort to provide for their security.

There is no way we will forget M.D. His magnetism, along with his model for ministry, will stay with us. His gentle spirit and kind manner have affected all of us who knew him and loved him.

Reverend O'Neil Mackey, Sr.
Presiding Elder
Brooklyn/Westchester District
New York Annual Conference AMEC